SKI SPOTS
ALPE

Original concept by **Francis Johnston**
Original photography by the author, unless otherwise credited
Front cover photography courtesy of Neilson Active Holidays

Produced by the Bridgewater Book Company
Project Editor: Emily Casey Bailey
Project Designer: Lisa McCormick

Published by Thomas Cook Publishing
PO Box 227, The Thomas Cook Business Park, Unit 15/16, Coningsby Road,
Peterborough PE3 8SB, United Kingdom
email: books@thomascook.com
www.thomascookpublishing.com
+44 (0) 1733 416477

First edition © 2005 Thomas Cook Publishing
Text © 2005 Thomas Cook Publishing; Maps © 2005 Thomas Cook Publishing
ISBN-13: 978-1-84157-513-1
ISBN-10: 1-841575-13-5
Head of Thomas Cook Publishing: Chris Young
Project Editor: Kelly Anne Pipes
Production/DTP: Steven Collins

Snowsports and related activities have an inherent level of danger and carry
a risk of personal injury. They should be attempted only by those with a full
understanding of these risks and with the training/experience to evaluate them,
or under the personal supervision of suitably qualified instructors or mountain
guides. Mountain conditions are highly variable and change quickly – weather
and avalanche risk level conditions must be carefully considered.

ACKNOWLEDGEMENTS
This book is dedicated to Sofia Barbas and all my family. It is the result of many wonderful days and nights in the mountains, aided by and accompanied by some great characters. Specific thanks go to Marie-Hélène Pascal and Audrey Robert at the Office du Tourisme de l'Alpe d'Huez; Ailbhe Pounau at SATA; Stephan Corporon at the Comité Départemental du Tourisme de l'Isère; Mike Stoker at Salomon Sports; Phillip Simpson, for his on-site research, notes and photography for the Montfrais area, Signal/Villard-Reculas and Oz-en-Oisans sectors; and to Sofia for research assistance and for compiling the Language section.

CONTENTS

SYMBOLS KEY

The following is a key to the symbols used throughout this book:

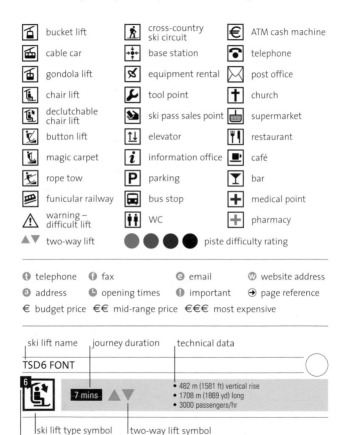

🔲	bucket lift	🚶	cross-country ski circuit	€	ATM cash machine
🚡	cable car	⧈	base station	☎	telephone
🔲	gondola lift	✗	equipment rental	✉	post office
🔲	chair lift	🔧	tool point	✝	church
🔲	declutchable chair lift	🔲	ski pass sales point	🔲	supermarket
🔲	button lift	⬆⬇	elevator	🍴	restaurant
🔲	magic carpet	*i*	information office	☕	café
🔲	rope tow	P	parking	Y	bar
🔲	funicular railway	🚌	bus stop	✚	medical point
⚠	warning – difficult lift	🔲	WC	✚	pharmacy
▲▼	two-way lift	●●●●	piste difficulty rating		

🔵 telephone   🔵 fax   🔵 email   🔵 website address

🔵 address   🔵 opening times   🔵 important   ➔ page reference

€ budget price   €€ mid-range price   €€€ most expensive

---

ski lift name   journey duration   technical data

TSD6 FONT

6 🔲	7 mins ▲▼	• 482 m (1581 ft) vertical rise • 1708 m (1869 yd) long • 3000 passengers/hr

ski lift type symbol   two-way lift symbol

number of passengers

INTRODUCTION TO SKISPOTS

Welcome to SkiSpots, an innovative series of specialist guidebooks to Europe's top ski regions, designed and compiled by some of Europe's most experienced snowsports professionals. Whether you ski, board, blade or Langlauf, are a piste virgin or a seasoned powder hound, SkiSpots are as indispensable as your ski pass.

With a snowsports-centric layout and a snowsports-specific information flow, these guides are focused on the major linked ski domains and the resorts that access them: with historical snowfall charts and analysis as a guide to the best dates to visit for optimum snow conditions; base station layouts and resort street plans; detailed information and critiques on all principal ski lifts and pistes; ideas for alternative activities and après ski; and complemented by the history, culture, gastronomy, language and attractions of the surrounding region.

Action-packed and filled with insider intelligence and technical expertise, with a wealth of general information to keep non-skiers interested too, SkiSpots are the next best thing to having a private mountain guide.

On a piste map, the sun is always shining, the snow is always powder perfect, the visibility is always excellent and the links are always open. SkiSpots provide an invaluable extension to your piste map, describing the ski area in three dimensions, clarifying ambiguous and complicated routes, directing you away from the links that don't work and towards the areas that will deliver the most satisfying descents.

The author has visited every corner of the resorts and ski domains, taken and timed every lift, skied every piste and most of the powder fields in between and visited every recommended bar and restaurant – it's a dirty job, but someone's got to do it!

Snow excites a childlike fascination in us all; who hasn't felt the urge to rush out and throw a snowball after even the slightest frosting of this magical powder on a crisp winter morning? The first priority of this guidebook is to stimulate your excitement about the mountains, striving to inform and nourish your enjoyment of this wonderful environment and direct you to the best that the resorts and ski areas have to offer.

The first part of the book gives you a flavour of the region you are visiting, detailing the history of the area and the pioneering beginnings of the extensive snowsports infrastructure that you enjoy today; with an overview on the regional food and drink and a basic snowsports-centric vocabulary in the local language to help you engage more readily with your hosts and speed up assistance if and when you require it.

The second part of the guide begins with an all-important briefing on the dangers of the mountains in winter, and the tried-and-tested ways of minimizing the risks to which you expose yourself when participating in adventure sports in this environment; together with the rules and regulations that all slope users have to observe. Next comes the introduction to each major resort and ski area and how to access them; with street plans, piste maps and ski area data; ski pass information, resort transport, equipment hire, ski schools, childcare, resort and ski area services; plus snowfall history charts. Each sector of the ski area is then broken down by base station layout, first access points and onward links, with a detailed lift-by-lift description and piste-by-piste critique; every mountain bar and restaurant is covered in depth and suggested point-to-point itineraries are illustrated to assist with route planning to help you squeeze the maximum potential out of your day.

When the après-ski begins, SkiSpots continue with you by suggesting alternative activities and listing the cafés, restaurants, bars and clubs in which to round off your day. The book finishes with some ideas for days away from the pistes, together with an insight into the attractions of the region in summer.

www.ski-ride.com

Due to the ephemeral nature of snow, and the dynamic nature of the mountain environment and the snowsports industry, resort facilities and ski area boundaries can change. Therefore the SkiSpots series is also supported by an Internet portal, delivering up-to-the-minute news and links to the ski areas: on-site webcams, live snow reports and current weather information, resort fact sheets, events diary, tour operator links and much more, enhancing both this guidebook and your trip.

HOW TO USE THIS BOOK

SkiSpots travel guides give ski lift and piste information in a unique graphical format. Detailed information is given on the type of ski lift, journey duration, capacity, directions to follow on arrival and onward links. All principal pistes are covered and are colour-coded by level of difficulty with detailed access routes, descriptions of terrain, best lines of descent and onward links, accompanied by regular piste map illustrations to help you in real-time itinerary planning and route-finding on-the-move.

Point-to-point route-finder information is not necessarily the quickest option, but rather the best on-piste direction to deliver the most enjoyable route between the specified points. The route-finders are detailed for both competent novices and good intermediates.

ABOUT THE AUTHOR

Francis (Gary) Johnston was born in County Down, Northern Ireland. He was previously employed at a senior level with two of the UK's leading Ski, Lakes & Mountains tour operators, having lived and worked in Andorra, Spain and Portugal. He has also worked in or visited most of the leading French, Austrian and Italian ski resorts, having personally accompanied and guided well over four thousand visitors and travel industry professionals during that time.

Francis now divides his time between Andorra, France and Brighton in England, travelling up to six months each year in the Alps and Pyrenees.

❶ The Alpine environment can be harsh and dangerous, but it is also very fragile – please respect it and leave nothing but your tracks in the snow.

REGIONAL
INTRODUCTION
Isère

WELCOME – BIENVENUE

Alpe d'Huez lies in the Oisans area of France's Isère département; a land of diverse physical contrasts which straddles the boundary between the Northern and Southern Alps. Over 60 distinct types of landscape have been classified in Isère – the greatest number for any area in France, ranging from sun-drenched arable plains and fertile river valleys to sheer escarpments and deep caverns; rolling wooded hills and lush high-altitude meadows to classically-shaped Alpine peaks and glacial deserts. This land also has a rich human landscape, filled with history and tradition; a land where respect and enthusiasm for local customs and culture are protected and encouraged, preserving much of the original charm of the region and adding to its already strong appeal as a world-class mountain-holiday destination.

Isère's capital Grenoble is an Olympic city and regarded as the capital of the French Alps; along with Innsbruck in Austria it is one of the most populous and important cities in this backbone of Europe. Stendal (pseudonym of Henri Beyle, 1783–1842, author of *Le Rouge et le Noir*) was a native of the city and described it as having 'a mountain at the end of every street'; despite its lofty surroundings, the city paradoxically also has the distinction of being France's flattest city, spread out at the wide confluence point of the Isère and Drac rivers. It houses one of Europe's oldest universities and has one of France's largest student/resident ratios, infusing the city with a young and vibrant atmosphere. In contrast to its long and illustrious past, the city and its environs are now a thrusting technological heartland, often referred to as the 'Silicon Valley of France'.

◀ Grenoble: 'a mountain at the end of every street'

SNOWSPORTS PEDIGREE

Isère's ski stations jockey for position in snowsports' premier league: Chamrousse in the Chaine de Belledonne, just outside Grenoble, hosted the 1968 Winter Games; the Vercors Massif is a mecca for Nordic ski enthusiasts, boasting over 800 km (500 miles) of cross-county trails; and the towering glacial massifs of the Grandes Rousses and Ecrins, south-east of Grenoble, are home to Alpe d'Huez and Les Deux Alpes – the former, one of Europe's largest linked ski domains and the latter focused around Europe's largest skiable glacier.

Despite their southern latitude, these resorts are also at high enough altitudes to guarantee a long ski season and are blessed with favourable microclimates that ensure sufficiently regular snowfalls. The influence of the south is still felt though in the stability of the local weather patterns and, when not snowing, the skies above the slopes are often bluebird clear and provide first-rate visibility.

The extent of the ski areas means that there is something here for everyone, from nervous novices to experienced adrenaline junkies, and the Oisans resorts are some of France's, and therefore the world's, best all-round snowsports destinations.

STATISTICS
- 36 ski stations, 13 of which are 'internationally classified'
- 20 resorts specializing in Nordic skiing
- A total of 445 ski lifts across the region's resorts
- More than 2500 km (1563 miles) of pistes
- Further info: www.isere-tourisme.com and www.oisans.com

REGIONAL IDENTITY

The Celtic and Gallic tribes that founded the earliest settled communities in these high and harsh Alpine valleys included the Vocontii and the fierce Allobroges, who fought alongside Vercingétorix the Gaul, but from 121 BC onwards they gradually succumbed to the might of the Roman Empire. Burgundian tribes from the Rhine that were compliant to Rome were allowed to settle in their place, around present-day Grenoble and Chambéry, and the area began to develop as a defined region. After the fall of the Roman Empire, the territory became part of the Kingdom of Burgundy and was subject to frequent changes of fortune following various conflicts during the next five centuries. Burgundy was eventually incorporated into the Holy Roman Empire in 1032 and the vast kingdom was split into feudal superstates, corresponding more or less with present-day Savoie, Provence and Isère.

To the north, Savoie rose to become one of the most politically powerful states in Europe, ruling over the key Alpine passes and much of north-west Italy; to the south, Provence was controlled by the commercially astute Catalan Counts of Forcalquier, Toulouse and Barcelona; whilst the large, strategically important, buffer state between these two dynamic neighbours came under the dominion of the Counts of Albon. It is this latter extensive territory that corresponds with present-day Isère.

THE DAUPHINÉ

One of the most influential of the Albons, Guigues IV, had Dauphin as his second name and his county became known as the Dauphiné in his honour, with each successive ruler adopting the title of Dauphin; the Isère region is still recognized by this ancient sobriquet to the present day.

In the 14th Century, the Dauphin Humbert II founded Grenoble university; he was an extravagant patron of the arts and benefactor of the church, spending lavish amounts on grandiose cultural projects. His participation in the crusades to the Holy Land drained his already dwindling state coffers to such an extent that upon his return in 1349 he abdicated and sold the Dauphiné to Philippe VI of Valois, King of France; the title of Dauphin was then conferred on the heir to the French throne.

THE FRENCH REVOLUTION

In 1447, the Dauphin Louis II (the future King Louis XI) established his court in the Dauphiné, abolished the feudal system and established the Parliament of Grenoble. Unfortunately this early example of local government didn't find favour with future kings and many political institutions were forcibly re-centralized back to the French crown. This erosion of democracy caused nation-wide civil discontent, which became focused by events developing in the Dauphiné: on 21 July 1788, the États du Dauphiné (the regional assembly) met at the Château de Vizille south-east of Grenoble. After a marathon full-day meeting, the assembly ratified a resolution which registered disapproval at the king's meddling in politics and his suppression of Parliament; it demanded a conference of all of the nation's regional assemblies and recognition of individual freedom for all French citizens. The assembly's resolution matched the national zeitgeist and unrest came to a head a year later after the king proscribed the regional assemblies altogether and attempted to ban the recently self-declared National Assembly. The inhabitants of most French cities rebelled; in Paris the Bastille was stormed and the whole nation rose against the monarchy and aristocracy.

Isère is thus regarded as the cradle of the French Revolution and the Château de Vizille (see page 249) today houses France's only specialized museum dedicated to this pivotal period of French history.

In 1791, the aristocratic provinces were broken up and the Dauphiné was divided up into three départements: Isère, Drôme and Hautes-Alpes.

ROUTE NAPOLEON

Napoleon I, on his return from exile on Elba in 1815, crossed the Southern Alps with a small army of supporters and passed into Isère via Corps and La Mure. At Laffrey, just 6 km (3¾ miles) south of Vizille, he encountered the troops of Louis XVIII at the historic 'meeting of the praire', where he famously won the hearts and minds of his would-be opposition by walking straight up to them and baring his chest, inviting them to shot him there and then if they truly didn't believe in his right to lead them as Emperor again. In recognition of Napoleon's past military glories in the expansion of the French Empire, the royal troops switched allegiance and marched side-by-side with him towards Grenoble. Present-day travellers in this region can follow the way-marked route of his eventually triumphant return, known as The Route Napoleon.

TOWARDS THE PRESENT DAY

In the mid-19th century, research by Louis Vicat (1786–1861) into Roman construction technology lead to the rediscovery of the process of cement production. The extensive calcareous deposits in the valleys around Grenoble proved to be an ideal raw material for the process, prompting an industrial boom for the region and driving the expansion of Grenoble into the Romanche valley.

Dauphiné cement became a major export earner and many of New York's earliest skyscrapers were constructed using it. Coal mining and paper milling were the other two big primary industries fuelling the prosperity of the region as a whole, whilst slate quarrying in the Vénéon valley contributed specifically to the economic wealth of the Oisans area and remained an important industry there right up to the outbreak of World War II.

During the war, the Resistance were particularly active throughout Isère, with Grenoble regarded as the 'capital of the maquis'. The reprisals and general destruction of the Nazi occupation had a terrible effect on the region however, and it was left weakened both demographically and economically.

Following the war, many fertile Alpine foothills and river valleys were established as agricultural areas, specializing in dairy products and fruit cultivation, but the most dramatic reversal of fortunes resulted from the rapid development of hydroelectricity, fuelling the advancement of related industries such as electrometallurgy and electrochemistry in the valleys around Grenoble. The historic university of Grenoble became an important centre of study for these technologies, as well as nuclear science, and the campus is still regarded today as one the most important research and development centres in Europe.

The steady growth of the mountain tourist industry also contributed to Isère's return to the world stage: the first tourist office in France was created in Grenoble, the surrounding mountains of the Chaine de Belledonne and Grandes Rousses and the Glaciers du Monts-de-Lans were developed as international ski stations and in 1968 the city hosted the Winter Olympics, centred on the Belledonne resort of Chamrousse, with the bobsleigh event held at Alpe d'Huez.

ALPE D'HUEZ

Evidence of a settled community of the Uceni peoples in the village of Huez dates the village's existence to 300–200 BC. Villagers survived by growing hardy crops and by keeping dairy animals. The wide, open meadows high above the village supported the community's herds during the summer and a small secondary hamlet of dwellings and barns was established on these higher altitude pastures. In French, the word 'alpe' refers to a mountain meadow, normally meant to mean a pasture for grazing livestock, hence the name l'Alpe d'Huez. During the long winter, the upper hamlet was left to hibernate and the inhabitants returned, with their animals, to the slightly more sheltered main village.

In the Middle Ages, a silver mine was opened on the hillside near to the present-day Altiport, supplying the Dauphin's mint at Grenoble and worked by miners who built the small village of Brandes-en-Oisans around the workings. The site of the mine and the village is an important archeological site and is recognized as a national historic monument. The site was discovered in 1899 by Hippolyte Muller, eminent archeologist and founder of the Musée Dauphinois. His work is recorded in a fascinating collection of photographs, notes and finds on display in the Musée d'Huez et de l'Oisans in the Vieil Alpe quarter of Alpe d'Huez (see page 65).

The villagers of Huez continued their subsistence farming on the meadows during the short summers and in the winter months they became peddlers and travelled throughout central and eastern France. A seam of anthracite was discovered on the flanks of Pic Blanc and the Mine de l'Herpie provided additional work and income for the population, which by then had grow to number around 300 people; but when an avalanche swept the miners bunkhouses away, the mine was never reopened.

SKI HISTORY

The better opportunities and easier life of the more modern and prosperous lowland towns and cities drew most of the younger inhabitants away to escape the harsh mountain existence. Then, in the early 1900s, a remarkable reversal of fortunes changed the social and economic dynamics of Huez: the newly fashionable sport of skiing altered the once negative perceptions of local climatic conditions, which gradually began to be recognized as one of the area's most valuable assets. A small hotel was opened in 1911 and the local primary school teacher Marie Muller is credited with having introduced the first skis to the village. During World War I, soldiers trained as Alpine troops in the area and helped develop the sport of skiing and its related equipment; the town is still a base for the French military today.

In 1926, a main road was constructed all the way up to Alpe d'Huez and the focus of attention turned away from the original village of Huez towards development of the upper village quarters on the alpe, with the mission of establishing a fully-serviced mountain-sports resort.

Jean Pomagalski, founder of the famous Poma ski lift design and construction company, built the world's first declutching drag lift in Alpe d'Huez in the autumn of 1936. The lift, which was just 50 m (55 yd) long, was constructed with wooden pylons and lift poles and served what became known as the 'Idiots piste' on the town slopes at l'Eclose (the site of the lift is still marked there by a modern button lift of the same name). In the same year, the resort's tourist office was founded and the number of hotel rooms increased to 245. A year later the resort's first ski school was formed, marking Alpe d'Huez's debut as a truly international ski resort.

EXPANSION

The ski slopes above the nearby village of Villard-Reculas were linked with those of Alpe d'Huez in 1946, and the ski area also began to expand higher up the flanks of Pic Blanc. A chair lift to the 2700 m (8856 ft) level was opened in 1956 and the SATA company was formed in 1958 to manage all future developments of the ski area's infrastructure. The burgeoning ski domain eventually reached the summit of Pic Blanc with the construction of a chair lift to the 3330 m (10,922 ft) level in 1962; two years later the Pic Blanc Tunnel was opened to allow skiers on the Glacier de Sarenne to reach the southern side of the massif again and to return to resort on-piste.

Auris-en-Oisans was linked in 1972, adding greatly to the extent of skiable terrain; to control the increased influx of skiers from so many satellite bases, SATA introduced the first ski pass in 1975. Until then, as was the case in most ski resorts, the lifts and slopes were operated on a pay-as-you-go basis.

The world's longest Alpine ski piste, the Sarenne run, was opened in 1976 and has remained as one of Alpe d'Huez's signature features. A massive programme of infrastructure improvements during the 1980s resulted in the construction of state-of-the-art cable cars, gondola lifts and snowmaking equipment, consolidating the station's position as a major international ski resort.

Vaujany was finally connected to the ski area in 1990, completing the links with the satellite stations, but by no means ending the expansion and ongoing improvements to the ski area and its supporting services, which continue apace to the present day. The Grandes Rousses domain is now amongst the world's top twenty ski areas for sheer extent and variety of pistes.

TRADITIONAL MOUNTAIN FARE

Regional gastronomy has too often been regarded as of secondary importance in the snowsports holiday experience. Now, however, more travellers are seeking to complement their time in the mountains with great meals too. The rich diversity of European regional cuisine is nowhere more enjoyable than in the actual regions that created it.

● *Produce of the Isère region*

France consistently lives up to its reputation as the world's foremost provider of gourmet food and fine wine and you could read a whole library of books on French gastronomy alone. The produce and specialities of Isère have a history and tradition intertwined with those of neighbouring Savoie; narrowing the focus to the specialities of these two départements should give you a flavour of the rich tradition of wholesome mountain cooking that is alive and well in these important Alpine regions.

With very little mountain land area suitable for intensive farming, surviving the harsh high altitude winters through history required a rustic, hearty diet which made full use of the limited range of indigenous foodstuffs. Isère mountain cuisine was therefore born out of necessity, relying heavily on dairy products from cows, goats and sheep; meat; game; a few hardy fruit and vegetable crops; together with cured and dried foodstuffs harvested and preserved during the summer and autumn.

REGIONAL PRODUCE

chou: Savoy cabbage; probably the most internationally renowned vegetable from the French Alps and a real staple of the local diet

coings: quinces; acidic pear-shaped fruit. These are popular mountain fruits because they are quite hardy and flourish where softer fruit would struggle. An important source of vitamin C in a mountain diet and used to make preserves and desserts such as rissoles – quince paste spread on cornmeal fingers and then baked or deep-fried and served warm sprinkled with sugar

poires: pears; Conference, Williams and Général Leclerc are the three most common and easily recognized varieties of the half-a-dozen regional favourites. The fresh Savoie fruit and juice carries an *Indication Géographique Protégée* (IGP) label protected by EU law and guaranteeing provenance from particular regions

pommes: apples; Golden Delicious, Jonagold, Elstar, Melrose and Idared are the most common among the dozen or so preferred varieties grown in this and the neighbouring Savoie region

pommes de terre: potatoes; a staple of the Isère diet ever since they were introduced into the Dauphiné province from the neighbouring Duchy of Savoie, long before either were part of France

noix de Grenoble: walnuts of Grenoble. Nuts form an important part of the high altitude mountain diet, being easy to store, long keeping, and packed with energy. They are used in everything: bread, starters, main courses and desserts. Walnut by-products are numerous and include walnut oil, jam and confectionery. Walnuts have been an emblematic product of Isère since the eleventh century and Grenoble walnuts were awarded an *Appellation d'Origine Contrôlée* (AOC – see page 27) in 1938. The principal areas of cultivation are located along the Isère valley west of Grenoble, particularly around Vinay and in the Sud-Grésivaudan region

DAIRY PRODUCTS

🔺 *'Tomme' cheese from Savoie*

Dairy herds play a major part in the gastronomic heritage of the Isère and Savoie, and their produce brims with the flavour and goodness of this pure environment. Alpine-specific breeds of cattle, mostly Abondance and Tarine, are pastured on the high-altitude meadows during the short Alpine summer from mid-June to early September. The meadows are watered by the glacial runoffs. Individual farm herds are usually quite small, but in late spring are combined with the cattle from neighbouring farms for the transhumance (transfer) up to the meadows as soon as the snows have cleared.

Chevrotin goats have also been farmed in these regions for many centuries and the Savoie Chevrotin cheese carries an AOC. Like the cattle, the goats are subject to a transhumance every spring to the high-altitude meadows, though the goats range much further and higher. Milking takes place two times each day and the cheese-making process is still mainly carried out by hand on-site in high-altitude barns.

CHEESES

Saint-Marcellin: this is, by tradition, a goat's milk cheese, but nowadays it is made using a milder blend of goat's and cow's milk. The first historic mention of Saint-Marcellin cheese dates from the 15th century: on the occasion of a hunt, the Dauphin Louis II, the future King Louis XI, was injured and was looked after

QUALITY GUARANTEES

Indication Géographique Protégée (IGP): established by the European Commission to protect geographic names applied to agricultural products, such as Savoie apples and pears

Label Régional Savoie: a guarantee of provenance from the Savoie region and, by association, a guarantee of quality

Appellation d'Origine Contrôlée (AOC): official provenance and quality guarantee protected by European Commission law. AOC recognizes and protects the specific characteristics inherent in regional produce as a subtle and unreproducable blend of geographic position, reputation, tradition and knowledge passed down from generation to generation, producing a unique set of circumstances which impart a peculiar quality to the product. Corresponds to the Europe-wide *Appellation d'Origine Protégée* (AOP), protected designation of origin law. A guarantee of provenance from a particular region and, by association, a guarantee of production quality, rigorous selection process and traceability.

by local woodcutters, who gave him some cheese to eat. Louis proclaimed it delicious and Saint-Marcellin became a regular feature on the table of the French king

Bleu de Vercors-Sassenage: AOC; a medium-strength creamy blue cheese produced since the Middle Ages by the farmers of the Vercors, originally as a tax paid to the Lord of Sassenage. It is often used in *fondue savoyarde*

Tomme de Belledonne: in the regional dialects, the word Tomme simply means 'cheese', but also refers to the mould in which the cheeses are pressed. A medium-hard cheese with small holes and a rich creamy taste. It is now promoted as an organic product (*agriculture biologique*)

◓ *Isère dairy favourites*

Reblochon AOC: strong-smelling soft cheese made with milk from Abondance cattle, which is pressed into hand-sized rounds. One of the prime ingredients of *tartiflette* (see page 33), this cheese is made traditionally from the sweeter second milking (the *rebloche*) and has a recorded history dating back to the 13th century

Beaufort AOC: known as the 'Prince of Gruyères', this is a strong hard cheese moulded into large rounds using beechwood hoops, which not only maintain the shape but also give the cheese its distinctive concave edge. Beaufort has a delicate ivory colour but the flavour is strong. Used in *fondue savoyarde* and in gratin dishes, but equally well-suited to simple presentation in a cheese-board selection

Emmental de Savoie: cow's milk cheese with a rich, creamy interior and smooth with well-distributed holes. Traditionally ripened for 75 days and awarded a Savoie label

Chevrotin AOC: goat's milk cheese mostly from the Aravis area of Haute Savoie, around the ski resort of La Clusaz. Produced exclusively on individual farms, not collectives

Tamié: a fine cow's milk cheese produced by Trappist monks near Albertville; its packaging is instantly recognizable as it bears the Maltese cross

CURED MEATS & SAUSAGES

Ham (*jambon*) and cured sausages (*salaisons*) are staples of the Alpine diet, as they are an excellent way to preserve meat for the long winters. The most typical regional ham is the mildly salted *jambon de Savoie* , a dry-cured mountain ham similar to Parma ham, which is aged for at least 9–12 months and served in wafer-thin slices as a starter. Also try the lamb hams from the area around the ski resort of Valloire.

There seem to be as many varieties of cured sausages throughout these regions as there are choices of cheese in the whole of France! Isère and Savoie dry sausages are always made with natural casings, slowly aged and never frozen. They are served cold as starters and in salads, added to stews or simply grilled. The most popular include:

saucisses de Magland: cured sausage made with lean pork; typical of the Vallée de l'Arve

diots: small fresh meat sausages, made either solely with lean pork or with a mixture of pork and beef; normally cooked in white wine

caillettes: fresh minced pork sausages with green vegetables

pormoniers de Tarentaise: pork offal with leeks and herbs

saucissons d'ânes: sausages made with donkey meat. Goat meat is also often used

grelots: pork sausages with nuts

salaisons de Savoie: *salaisons* is simply a generic name for charcuterie, taken here to signify specialities from Savoie

🔺 *Sausages at a regional market*

FISH

The clear, pure mountain streams, rivers and lakes provide
an important source of protein in the Alpine diet.

char: delicate and succulent lake fish common in the Alpine lakes,
particularly Lac d'Annecy

lavaret and féra: commonly encountered as 'whitefish' on English
menu translations. Both are the same species (dace) but named
differently to distinguish the *lavaret* as the variety from the Lac
du Bourget or Lac d'Annecy, and *féra* from Lac Léman. Generally
served *à la meunière* (see page 31) or in a light cream sauce

truite: trout; fresh river trout, rather than farmed, is the most
prized and is stipulated as such on the menu

omble chevalier: a member of the salmon family, similar to
rainbow trout, which lives in deep, cold glacial lakes. A less
common, much prized fish with an excellent flavour

VEGETARIAN

It has to be said, vegetarians will have a hard time of it in the
mountains, vegans even more so. The concept of vegetarianism
still is not fully understood, or acceptably accommodated, even
in the largest hotels. You may have to resign yourself to picking
through salads and pizzas to remove anchovies, prawns and ham.

Most of the vegetarian options offered depend heavily on salads,
eggs and cheese, with the omelette being king. Buffets and self-
service restaurants are easiest, but they still rely on meat and fish
dishes for main courses; the only vegetarian option again usually
being an omelette – charged at the same price as the meat dish.

Crêpes, pasta and pizzas are all reliable options; raclette and
fondue are the best regional specialities suitable for vegetarians
(see page 33).

COOKING TECHNIQUES

Local recipes have assimilated the techniques and ingredients of neighbouring regions of Savoie, Lyonnais and Bresse, with hints of the Mediterranean; the Italian region of Piedmont (once part of Savoie) has also made a noticeable contribution. The following are a selection of the most popular and representative styles of cooking:

à la meunière: dipped in flour and fried in butter

au gratin: with grated cheese and often breadcrumbs. *Gratin de pommes de terre savoyard* (fine slices of potato and grated Beaufort cheese baked with butter and stock) is an energy-rich dish

à la bergère: 'shepherd style', generally meaning with ham, mushrooms, onion and very finely cut potatoes

à la bourguignonne: 'Burgundy style', generally meaning casseroled with red wine, onions and mushrooms, but also a style of fondue where meat is dipped in hot oil instead of the Savoie style where hot cheese is the dipping mix. *Fondue bourguignonne* includes a selection of sauces in which to dip the cooked meat

à l'italienne: using pasta and tomatoes

à l'ancienne: prepared to an old, very traditional recipe; used as a generic term with no set ingredients or method of cooking

à la lyonnaise: 'Lyon style', cooked with onions, usually a potato dish

à la niçoise: 'Nice style', usually applied to salad or pizza and including anchovies, tomatoes and olives in the ingredients; with French beans and egg too when referring to the salad

à la vigneron: 'wine grower style', generally any recipe involving wine in its key ingredients

à la crème: made with cream; that is, in a cream sauce

à la dauphinoise: potatoes baked in cream and/or milk, usually served *au gratin*; a classic speciality of the Isère region

WELL DONE

The French prefer meat rare (*bleu* or *saignante*), so if you prefer it to be well done (*bien cuit*) try asking for it to be very well done (*très bien cuit*), otherwise it is likely to arrive closer to medium (*à point*).

REGIONAL SPECIALITIES

A noble culinary heritage continues to pervade the region's kitchens and restaurants and tongue-twisting, tastebud-teasing local dishes, redolent of the rigours and pleasures of high altitude life, have survived and thrived. Pack your appetite along with your ski gear.

gratin dauphinois: the most emblematic dish of the Isère region. This cheese-topped dish of potatoes is mentioned for the first time in the Grenoble city archives (on 12 July 1788) on the menu of an official meal organized by the Duke of Clermont-Tonnerre, Lieutenant General of the Dauphiné. It consists of potatoes, whole milk, cream, salt, pepper, nutmeg, butter and garlic; originally it did not include grated cheese. The potatoes are cooked in the milk and cream, along with the seasonings, before being baked together in the oven to produce a rich and creamy comfort food – perfect as a winter energy booster

raviole: the *raviole* of Dauphiné are small squares of fine pasta, very similar to Italian ravioli, containing a filling of Tomme cheese, eggs and parsley. According to local tradition, proper *raviole* are poached in chicken broth rather than plain water

ganèfles: baked ravioli stuffed with cheese and served in a cream sauce. Bang goes the diet!

farcis: stuffed vegetables (usually minced pork) and cooked in stock

tartiflette: ubiquitous stable of Isère and Savoie chalet kitchens, resembling lasagne in appearance and served for lunch and/or for dinner. A blend of potatoes, Reblochon cheese, lardons, butter, onions, garlic and crème fraîche, oven-baked and served almost bubbling. Traditionally served with charcuterie and pickles. The Savoyard version is traditionally served in a pastry case resembling a large Yorkshire pudding

raclette: a half-wheel of smooth, firm raclette cheese served on a special little heater to melt the cheese, which you scrape off hot on to your plate or bread at the table. Usually served with potatoes and pickles

fondue: in Isère and Savoie this is usually the bread-dipped-in-hot-cheese version, so if you're vegetarian, be sure to order the cheese version rather than the meat-based (*fondue bourguignonne*) one. *Fondue savoyarde* is a blend of two or more cheeses and a little white wine, gently brought to near boiling to liquify, then served at your table in a pot with a flame burner to keep it hot. You are provided with chunks of bread and little spears to dip into the bubbling cheese mixture. Usually served with potatoes and/or salad and charcuterie

pierrade: small strips of meat cooked on a hot slate sprinkled with rock salt, this is usually another DIY task at your table; served with dips and salad

crozets: tiny squares of wheat pasta; sometimes blended with buckwheat flour (*crozets au sarrasin*)

potée savoyarde: stew; usually of ham and vegetables, generally always including Savoy cabbage and potatoes, simmered together but then served separately, with vegetable broth poured over toasted bread

polenta: made from milled corn which is pressed into thick sausage-shapes and used as a carbohydrate-loaded base for a wide range of dishes. Normally associated with the cuisine of the neighbouring Italian regions, but is in fact an ancient and important Savoie speciality. It is easy to store and an important source of energy during the long winter. Traditionally served with sausages or meats in sauce

farcement: similar to terrines and formed by pressing ingredients in a special mould. Recipes vary from village to village, even from house to house, but typically use potatoes and dried fruit grated and kneaded together then pressed into a mould lined with bacon, which is then cooked in a bain-marie for 3–4 hours. The dish is turned out and served in slices and has an unusual sweet-and-sour flavour. A particular favourite during harvests and transhumance periods, as the dish stores well and is packed with energy. The slices can be reheated quickly by sautéing in a pan

gâteau aux noix: walnut cake. A classic dessert of the Isère region, using the famous walnuts of Grenoble; very sweet, but with just the right touch of bitterness from the nuts

---

MENU

To see the menu, ask for *la carte*, as the 'menu' in France is taken to mean just the daily set menu.

Menu du jour: an economical set menu, usually two or three courses, with at least two choices, often with dessert, bread and sometimes even water and/or table wine included

---

▶ *Walnut cake, an Isère favourite for those with a sweet tooth*

MOUNTAIN SPORTS NUTRITION

Don't make the mistake of regarding eating on snowsports holidays as merely pit stops for refuelling: a couple of beers and a hamburger won't help you nail that three-sixty or give you the legs to progress into that fresh powder after lunch!

Nutritious, warming meals with quality, fresh ingredients and frequent non-alcoholic fluid intake are what your body craves at altitude. Remember, you are in an Arctic environment participating in a demanding sport. This requires an athletic-minded approach to diet. Far better to supply your body with optimum nutrition while, since you're on holiday, allowing yourself a more gourmet event. If you had a racehorse worth millions, you wouldn't feed it beer and hamburgers! So why treat yourself as any less worthy?

SUGGESTED SNOWSPORTS DIET

Breakfast: a 'Continental' breakfast of coffee, croissant and cigarette just isn't adequate to support a morning in the mountains – you need slow-release energy-rich foods such as muesli, bread with cheese or ham, honey and yogurt

Lunch: light, warm dishes based on pasta, rice or vegetables with meat or fish to supply plenty of complex carbohydrate energy, protein and fibre

Dinner: salad, soup or vegetables, followed by fish, fowl or light meat – don't make it too hearty as a heavy meal will interfere with your sleep

Snacks: fruit or yogurt or a sandwich or dried fruits/nuts

Drinks: fruit juice, tea (herbal is best), hot chocolate, water and more water

WINE

A giant in the oenological world, France needs no preamble regarding the quality of its wines.

The Isère region, though, is not a noted wine-growing region, with only the ancient Gallo-Roman area around the town of Vienne, just south of Lyon, beginning to emerge again as a serious wine-producing area. These ancient vineyards, situated on granite hillsides overlooking the town, had been abandoned along with many others in the region during the first half of the 20th century, following the phylloxera infestation which proved so widespread and devastating in Europe at that time. Isère's recently reborn wines, mostly produced with Syrah grapes, are still developing and should continue to improve as the new vines age. The wines tend to be strong: Sotanum and Taburnum are the names to look out for, particularly in regional speciality shops and delicatessens.

The Savoie region has been producing wine since Roman times and were referred to by Pliny (AD 23–79), who named them as the wines of Allobrogie; *vin de pays d'Allobrogie* is now the name used for good-quality table wines produced outside the AOC boundaries. The region boasts a diversity of terrain: from mountain foothills, river valleys and sunny lake shores.

The rich alluvial land of the Combe de Savoie in particular is a major wine producing area, boasting a number of world-class, yet relatively little-known labels, although the vast majority of wine produced in the region is for local consumption.

Mostly, Savoie wines are subtle whites. They should be drunk young and go very well with the delicate lake fish and creamy local cheeses; they are also used extensively in cooking, featuring as a key ingredient in *fondue savoyarde* to help liquify the cheese.

There are four principal AOCs and 22 Crus in Savoie: the AOCs are Vin de Savoie; Roussette de Savoie; Crépy; and Seyssel, which is the oldest of the AOCs, first awarded in 1942. All have the distinctive cross of Savoie moulded just below the neck of the bottle. The Vin de Savoie AOC is subdivided into Abymes, Apremont, Arbin, Ayze, Bergeron, Chautagne, Chignin, Cruet, Jongieux,

🔺 *Apremont, a classic Savoie white*

Marignan, Marin, Montmélian, Ripaille, St Jean de la Porte, St Jeoire Prieuré and Pétillant de Savoie. The Roussette de Savoie AOC is subdivided into Frangy, Marestel, Monterminod and Monthoux.

No fewer than 23 different varieties of grape are cultivated; three times more whites than reds, as the whites are best suited to the chalky soil.

WHITES

Jacquère: predominates in the Combe de Savoie and Les Abymes areas, used in Apremont and Abymes wines. Light dry white, with a very delicate yellow tint

Bergeron: almost exclusively grown in the Chignin Cru communes

Altesse: most common in the Seyssel and Frangy terroirs and used in AOC Roussette de Savoie. Legend states that a Cypriot royal introduced this variety from her homeland on her visit to Savoie

Chasselas: predominantly grown in the regions nearest to the Swiss border

Roussanne: mainly cultivated in the Chignin Cru

REDS

Mondeuse: the most prevalent Savoie red, mostly grown in the Combe de Savoie area. Produces wines with a rich purple-red hue, with a bouquet of strawberry, raspberry and violet. Good accompaniment with charcuterie

Pinot Noir: the classic red grape of Burgundy; here, some is used in the Chignin Vin de Savoie reds

Gamay: classic old-world vine (Beaujolais-lovers will recognize its fruity style) cultivated for its reliability

FRENCH WINE TERMS

Appellation d'Origine Contrôlée (AOC): the premier quality control, protected by law, awarded to the highest quality wines in specifically demarcated areas

Vin Délimité de Qualité Supérieure (VDQS): quality award just below full AOC

Vin de Pays: followed by the name of the département it comes from. Local table wine

Vin Doux Natural (VDN): naturally sweet wine (dessert wine).

cru: there are two distinct meanings to this term – it is used to refer to the specific territory where the wine comes from, but is also used as a standard of classification and is normally encountered with champagnes and fine wines which take the terms Premier Cru, Grand Cru and Premier Grand Cru, denoting the very highest quality wines

en carafe: decanted into a carafe, usually a half-litre or litre

en pichet: decanted into a jug; usually a small one, but available in various sizes to suit the number of people at your table

sec: dry; **moëlleux**: sweet; **pétillant** (or **perlé**): slightly sparkling; **mousseux**: sparkling

VIN CHAUD
Hot mulled wine. Ubiquitous après-ski warmer in Alpine ski resorts.
Recipe: *1 bottle (75 cl) red Vin de Savoie, 115 g (4 oz) sugar, 1 lemon, sprig of thyme, bay leaf, clove.*
Heat the wine and sugar in a saucepan; when the froth begins to form, remove from the heat, add the lemon (thinly sliced), and other ingredients. Return to the heat and allow to boil for no more than two minutes. Serve hot.

APERITIFS AND DIGESTIFS

Chartreuse: the most famous regional product from Isère, with a recorded history stretching back 400 years and made to a secret recipe by the monks from the Grande-Chartreuse monastery at Voiron, north of Grenoble. Green Chartreuse (55° proof) is the strongest; added to hot chocolate it is a delicious après-ski warmer. Yellow Chartreuse (40° proof) is sweeter and softer, it is made with the same plants as the green variety, but in different proportions

génépy: a generic term for all regional spirits using Alpine worm-wood plant in their flavouring. The liqueur is served as an aperitif and/or digestif and is used to flavour pastries and desserts

Gentian liqueur: flavoured with the intensely blue-coloured flower of the Alpine Gentian

liqueur de noix: liqueur made using the famous Grenoble walnuts; another product of the monastery of Grande-Chartreuse

antésite: a non-alcoholic concentrate of liquorice which you add to mineral water. First introduced over a century ago by a pharmacist from Voiron, and used to aid digestion

LIGHTER DRINKS

bière: beer. Most of the beers available in resort bars are standard international brews sold from the tap. However, the Brasserie Artisanale du Dauphiné is a notable local producer from Grenoble; look out for their Mandrin, walnut-flavoured beer, named after this region's own version of Robin Hood

café: with breakfast, as a mid-morning and afternoon pick-me-up, after dinner and at just about any other social encounter, a coffee is as much of a national institution in France as 'a nice cup of tea' is in the UK. The variations in preference are wide ranging: *décaféiné* is decaf; *café crème* is made with milk or cream and is more commonly referred to as *café au lait*; *café noir* is a small black coffee; *café express* is espresso. *Café crème/café au lait* is traditionally only drunk at breakfast time by the French, but at any time of day by tourists

tisane: herbal infusion; this is the generic term in French for any herbal tea

eau: water. The Alps have a plethora of natural springs which are the source of many brands of bottled water. Regionally, most comes from the Haute Savoie, from the springs at the foot of the Alps on the southern shores of Lac Léman, but bottled water from the spa town of Aix-les-Bains on the Lac du Bourget is an excellent local mineral water.

There are various types to choose from: *eau gazeuse* is sparkling; *eau plate* is still; *eau nature* is plain tap water; *eau minérale* is mineral water, such as Perrier or Evian, each from a specific source and high in mineral content and often with quite a distinct, even salty, taste.

Although tap water quality is generally excellent, it is safest to drink only bottled water.

DELICATESSENS & GOURMET SHOPS

Au Régal Paysan Alpe d'Huez delicatessen focusing on regional charcuterie products. ❸ Branches at avenue des Jeux and route de la Poste (the latter location is right next door to a good butcher shop and a shop that sells fondue sets and raclette heaters)

Jannin Lovely chocolaterie and patisserie with a wide range of regional gourmet food products and liqueurs. ❸ Avenue des Jeux, Alpe d'Huez

Aux Caprices des Neiges Bakery/patisserie which offers a large range of cakes, tarts and pastries; good for birthday cakes. ❸ Branches at place Joseph Paganon, l'Eclose Est and avenue de l'Etendard, Alpe d'Huez

La.Mi.Do.Ré Tiny regional products shop; local and Savoie cheeses, local honey and charcuterie; also sells sandwiches filled with the products on sale. ❸ Place Centre Village in Vaujany

L'Âtre du Vaujaniat Bakery/patisserie and regional products shop; ready-made raclettes and fondues to take away; fondue sets and raclette heaters available to loan. ❸ Galerie Marchande in the upper level of Vaujany

LANGUAGE

PARLEZ-VOUS FRANÇAIS? DO YOU SPEAK FRENCH?

Having even a basic insight into the language of the country you are visiting will help enormously in getting the maximum enjoyment from your stay; allowing you to engage more readily with your hosts and speeding up assistance if you need it.

Of course, French is the official language of the region, but most of the tourism service personnel you will encounter will speak and understand some English.

The following is a selection of useful words and phrases most frequently needed on a snowsports holiday:

ENGLISH	FRENCH
Hello	*Bonjour*
Good morning	*Bonjour*
Good afternoon	*Bon après-midi*
Good evening	*Bonsoir*
Good night	*Bon nuit*
Goodbye	*Au revoir*
See you soon	*À bientôt*
Please	*S'il vous plaît*
Thank you	*Merci*
Yes	*Oui*
No	*Non*
How are you?	*Comment allez-vous?*
Very well thank you	*Très bien merci*
I don't understand	*Je ne comprends pas*
Sorry	*Pardon*
How much?	*C'est combien?*
Give me...	*Donnez-moi...*
Where is?	*Où est?*
Where are?	*Où sont?*
When?	*Quand?*
Why?	*Pourquoi?*
Open	*Ouvert*
Closed	*Fermé*

ENGLISH	FRENCH		ENGLISH	FRENCH
Monday	*Lundi*		Twelve	*Douze*
Tuesday	*Mardi*		Thirteen	*Treize*
Wednesday	*Mercredi*		Fourteen	*Quatorze*
Thursday	*Jeudi*		Fifteen	*Quinze*
Friday	*Vendredi*		Sixteen	*Seize*
Saturday	*Samedi*		Seventeen	*Dix-sept*
Sunday	*Dimanche*		Eighteen	*Dix-huit*
Winter	*L'hiver*		Nineteen	*Dix-neuf*
Summer	*L'été*		Twenty	*Vingt*
One	*Un*		Thirty	*Trente*
Two	*Deux*		Forty	*Quarante*
Three	*Trois*		Fifty	*Cinquante*
Four	*Quatre*		Sixty	*Soixante*
Five	*Cinq*		Seventy	*Soixante-dix*
Six	*Six*		Eighty	*Quatre-vingts*
Seven	*Sept*		Ninety	*Quatre-vingt-dix*
Eight	*Huit*		Hundred	*Cent*
Nine	*Neuf*		First	*Le premier*
Ten	*Dix*		Second	*Le deuxième*
Eleven	*Onze*		Third	*Le troisième*

ENGLISH	FRENCH
PHRASES	
Do you speak English?	*Parlez-vous anglais?*
What time is it?	*Quelle heure est-il?*
I would like	*Je voudrais*
Could you show me	*Pouvez-vous me l'indiquer*
Could you help me	*Pouvez-vous m'aider*
Where are the toilets?	*Où sont les toilettes?*
I've lost...	*J'ai perdu...*

ACCIDENTS / SICKNESS / EMERGENCIES	
I don't feel well	*Je ne me sens pas bien*
I've had a fall	*Je suis tombé*
I'm dizzy	*J'ai des vertiges*
It hurts here	*J'ai mal ici*
There's been an accident	*Il y a eu un accident*
Doctor	*Médicin*
Dentist	*Dentiste*

ENGLISH	FRENCH
ACCIDENTS / SICKNESS / EMERGENCIES (CONTINUED)	
I've got...	*Je souffre de...*
Constipation	*Constipation*
Diarrhoea	*Diarrhée*
Stomach ache	*Mal d'estomac*
Sunstroke	*Coup de soleil*
Headache	*Mal de tête*
Earache	*Mal d'oreille*
Head	*Tête*
Arm	*Bras*
Wrist	*Poignet*
Hand	*Main*
Leg	*Jambe*
Ankle	*Cheville*
Foot	*Pied*
Eye	*Oeil*
Ear	*Oreille*
Condom	*Préservatif*
Suncream	*Crème solaire*
Tampons	*Tampons*

DIRECTIONS AND PLACES	
Left	*À gauche*
Right	*À droite*
Straight ahead	*Tout droit*
I've lost my way	*Je me suis égaré*
Supermarket	*Supermarché*
Tourist information	*Office de tourisme*
Phonebox	*Cabine téléphonique*
Post office	*La poste*
Post box	*Boîte aux lettres*
Postage stamp	*Timbre*

AT THE RESTAURANT	
Do you have a menu in English?	*Vous avez un menu en anglais?*
The wine list	*La carte des vins*
Dish of the day	*Plat du jour*
The bill	*L'addition*
Bottle	*Bouteille*

ENGLISH	FRENCH
AT THE RESTAURANT (CONTINUED)	
Corkscrew	*Tire-bouchon*
Toothpick	*Cure-dent*
Tumbler	*Verre*
Wineglass	*Verre*
Rosé	*Vin rosé*
Red wine	*Vin rouge*
White wine	*Vin blanc*
Beer	*Bière*
Draught beer	*Bière pression*
Water	*Eau*
White coffee	*Café au lait*
Beef	*Boeuf*
Bread	*Pain*
Butter	*Beurre*
Cheese	*Fromage*
Chicken	*Poulet*
Dessert	*Déssert*
Egg	*Oeuf*
Fish	*Poisson*
Ice cream	*Glace*
Lamb	*Agneau*
Meat	*Viande*
Poultry	*Volaille*
Roast	*Rôti*
Salad	*Salade*
Soup	*Potage*
Vegetables	*Légumes*

SKI TERMS	
I'd like a skipass	*Je voudrais un forfait de ski*
To rent	*Louer*
To ice skate/ice skates	*Patiner/Patins à glace*
Avalanche	*Avalanche*
Bindings	*Fixations*
Cable car	*Téléphérique*
Chair lift	*Télésiège*
Cross-country skiing	*Ski de fond*
Drag lift	*Téléski*
Gloves	*Gants*

ENGLISH	FRENCH
SKI TERMS (CONTINUED)	
Goggles	*Lunettes de ski*
Gondola	*Télécabine*
Mountain	*Montagne*
Passport photo	*Photo d'identité*
Ski boots	*Chaussures de ski*
Ski lessons	*Leçons de ski*
Ski poles	*Bâtons de ski*
Ski wax	*Fart à ski*
Skis	*Skis*
Socks	*Chaussettes*
Snowchains	*Les chaînes de neige*

TEMP:	°C	−25	−20	−15	−10	−5	0	5	10	15	20	25	30
	°F	−13	−4	5	14	23	32	41	50	59	68	77	86

CONVERSIONS	
DISTANCES	
Centimetres to inches	x 0.394
Inches to centimetres	x 2.540
Yards to metres	x 0.914
Metres to yards	x 1.094
Miles to kilometres	x 1.609
Kilometres to miles	x 0.621

AREA	
Acres to hectares	x 0.405
Hectares to acres	x 2.471

HEIGHT	
Metres to feet	x 3.281
Feet to metres	x 0.305

ACCURACY

Conversion formulas are rounded up to 3 decimal places, therefore, calculations may result in slight differences in practice.

HEALTH & SAFETY
Piste security

PREPARATION FOR SNOWSPORTS

It is all too easy in these times of low-cost travel and rapid communications to forget that you are travelling from a relatively benign temperate climate straight into Arctic conditions. Furthermore, you are going to be careering around this wild and inhospitable environment standing on two planks or a tray, moving at the speed of a car with not much more than a knitted beanie and a pair of padded gloves to protect you!

The only way to ensure your safety and get maximum enjoyment out of your trip is to have respect for the seriousness of the situation you are putting yourself in and prepare accordingly.

Preparation begins at home: join a gym, ride a bike or just walk further and more often. The best and safest skiers and snowboarders are fit ones.

Once in your resort, warm-up at the start of each day and after rest breaks. A few minutes' stretching and/or jogging on the spot will pay dividends in your ability to sustain activity and avoid injury.

Weather conditions in the high mountains change rapidly and dramatically, so dress for all eventualities – it is easier to cool down than it is to warm up. Most heat loss occurs through your head, so always wear a hat. In the tricks parks and when freeriding, wear a helmet – all the best riders do.

ESSENTIAL ITEMS

Carry the following items with you on the mountain:

- water
- sunblock for skin and lips
- a piste map
- spare clothing
- high-energy snacks
- basic first-aid kit

PROTECTING YOURSELF FROM THE EFFECTS OF ALTITUDE

Temperature is inversely proportional to altitude: the higher you go, the lower the temperature drops.

Every 100 m (328 ft) rise in altitude above sea level equates to a shift north of around 161 km (100 miles). By the time you get up to 2500 m (8203 ft) that's equivalent to going from London to the Arctic Circle.

Conversely, the sun's radiation increases with altitude. For every 100 metres you go up, solar UV intensifies by about two per cent; so at 2500 metres you are being fried twice as quickly as you would be on a Mediterranean beach.

On overcast and snowy days, the clouds only disperse the UV-rays but do not stop them. Sunscreens absorb a set percentage of the UV reaching you; only a total sunblock and technical eyewear will provide maximum protection. Do not forget that snow reflects the sunlight and UV-rays – make sure you protect under your chin, below and behind your ears, under your nose and your eyelids. Goggles provide all-round protection and enhanced visibility; sunglasses are fine for wearing on the terraces or strolling around a resort, but they are not sportswear. Wearing a hat not only keeps you warm, but protects you from sunstroke too.

Dehydration is a problem in all active sports. When you add an increase in altitude to the equation, the problem becomes compounded and potentially fatal. Dehydration leads to fatigue, and tiredness is the primary cause of most accidents, injury and hypothermia. The best way to ensure that you are well hydrated is to start that way and maintain a good fluid balance throughout the day. The trick is to sip water or isotonic fluids little and often. Invest in a hydration backpack or carry a couple of bottles of water with you.

GEAR SAFETY

Ski boots were not designed for walking on the piste. On steep slopes it is always safer to keep your skis or snowboard on. If you take them off and there is ice underfoot you will have even less control than you had with your gear on.

When you do take your gear off, make sure that it is secured. If your skis or board slide away they can severely injure or even kill someone in just the few seconds it takes for them to pick up velocity. Legally you are responsible: this is not an accident but an avoidable lack of care.

Put your gear in a rack if there is one available. If not, make sure you set your board down upside down so that your bindings dig into the snow. Skis should be set down with their brake legs digging into the snow or placed upright and rammed deep into the snow where they can't run away if they fall over. Do not lean gear on the sides of cable car cabins or on flat walls. It will slide off and knock others with them and they are just like a guillotine when they crash down.

AU DELÀ DE CE PANNEAU VOUS ENTREZ DANS
UN DOMAINE HORS PISTE À VOS RISQUES ET PÉRILS
NI BALISE - NI SÉCURITÉ - NI PATROUILLE

THIS IS WHERE THE SKI SLOPES END
CONTINUE AT YOUR OWN RISK
NO MARKERS - NO BARRIERS - NO PATROLS

AN DIESEM SCHILD ENDEN DIE PISTEN
WEITERFAHRT AUF EIGENE GEFAHR
KEINE MARKIERUNGEN - KEINE ABSICHERUNG - KEINE PATROUILLEN

AVALANCHE RISK WARNINGS

Plain yellow flag = risk levels 1 to 2:
low to moderate probability of avalanche

Chequered yellow and black flag = risk levels 3 to 4:
moderate to high probability of avalanche

Black flag = risk level 5:
absolute risk of large avalanches

❶ Zero risk does not exist! Always be aware and prepared.

OFF-PISTE

❶ Check if your insurance policy covers off-piste skiing then follow these rules for optimum safety:

• Never leave the marked ski area on your own; it is safest to travel in groups of three persons minimum.

• Unless you know the area like the back of your hand, always employ a qualified mountain guide.

• Never blindly follow someone else's tracks, they may lead in the wrong direction or even off a cliff!

• Always carry the essential off-piste kit: avalanche transceiver, shovel, probe, map and compass.

If travelling off-piste in glacial areas you should also carry a climbing rope, harness, ice screws, carabiners and rope ascenders/foot slings. However, these items are only effective if you know what they are for and how to use them properly. Many resorts run avalanche awareness and safety equipment training courses. The golden rule is: get wise or get lost!

◀ *Piste signs and markers have been put there by mountain professionals – respect them! They are there to protect you and others too*

SLOPE RULES & REGULATIONS

The International Ski Federation (FIS) has set rules for slope users, which have established a legal precedent. Failure to abide by these rules may result in your ski pass being annulled and you may be banned from using the installations and the slopes. If you cause injury or death you may also be charged with negligence or manslaughter. The following is a summary:

1. Slope users must not endanger others.
2. You must adapt speed and behaviour to your ability and to current conditions.
3. The slope user in front always has priority.
4. When overtaking, leave room for those in front to manoeuvre.
5. Check uphill and downhill before you enter, start or cross pistes.
6. Only stop at the sides of the piste. If you have fallen, clear the slope quickly.
7. When moving up or down on foot, keep to the side of the piste.
8. Respect all piste signs and station information.
9. In the case of accidents, always give assistance.
10. You must give your identity to the Piste Patrol, Emergency Services and other accident victims when requested.

INSURANCE

Accident insurance is not included in ski pass prices. Make sure you are adequately covered or take the insurance supplement. Never travel without comprehensive winter sports travel insurance and always ensure that you are covered for on-mountain rescue and transport to hospital, on top of medical treatment and hospitalization cover. Some sports, such as paragliding and snowmobiling, are not covered by standard ski insurance and you will need to take out extra cover for these.

ALPE D'HUEZ /
GRANDES ROUSSES

Ski domain

INTRODUCTION

Welcome to the snowsports 'Island in the Sun', floating high above the sea of clouds in the Grandes Rousses Massif in France's Oisans region, previously a powerful and independent royal region owned by the heirs to the French crown.

The French national weather service records an average of 300 full days of sunshine per annum in Alpe d'Huez, with an average of seven and a half hours of sunshine per day in December, stretching to eleven in April. Centred on a glacial peak and high-altitude slopes, this privileged climate results in skiing's consummate combination of vibrant blue skies, perfect visibility and snow-sure conditions for the majority of the winter season.

This is the biggest and most important ski area in the Isère département, made up of a large modern resort surrounded by a five small traditional villages linked into the core ski domain. The area primarily appeals and is ideally suited to beginners to good intermediates, but with the huge variety of accessible terrain there is something here to keep all abilities interested. The jewel in the crown is the Sarenne black run which, at just over 16 km (10 miles) long, is the world's longest piste, providing a challenging summit-to-valley descent lasting over a hour before you need to take another ski lift.

PRONUNCIATION

Alpe d'Huez	Alp~do~hwez	**Huez**	Hwez
Auris	Or~ees	**Vaujany**	Vo~jaun~nay

◀ *Alpe d'Huez from the Signal de la Grande Sure*

Alpe d'Huez is a sprawling town with a substantial year-round population and strong commercial links with the Ile de France region around Paris, only four hours away by car, so its infrastructure is extensive and its ambiance vibrant and cosmopolitan. It offers a wide range of accommodation, a good selection of shops and a plethora of bars and restaurants. The excellent municipal sports and leisure facilities can be accessed for free by all holders of a current full area ski pass, and the resort has plenty of attractions and distractions for non-skiing visitors, making it an excellent choice for families and mixed-ability groups.

The area offers a choice of holiday bases, either in the buzzing main resort or in one of the tranquil satellite stations.

SATELLITE STATIONS & SKI SECTORS

The five satellite village stations (Auris-en-Oisans, Huez, Villard-Reculas, Oz-en-Oisans and Vaujany) are spread out at the foot of the Grandes Rousses Massif, and each offers a laid-back holiday experience where the pace of life is relatively slow and the welcome is warm and homely. All of the satellites are lift-linked into the core ski area, and all have 'home-run' pistes allowing for end-of-day descents to the resort, although a final short gondola lift is required to reach Vaujany.

Huez, Villard-Reculas and Vaujany offer the most authentic Oisans mountain village atmosphere and surroundings, the latter being quite a classy little micro-resort with fast, modern cable cars linking directly into the upper Alpe d'Huez ski area almost as quickly as the central resort's lifts.

The individual sectors that make up this large, linked ski domain also all have their own distinct character, providing a different experience with each day's skiing.

The **Auris sector** is quite extensive and could compete on its own with some smaller regional stations. This integrally complete ski area covers the full gamut of pistes for all abilities.

The uppermost **Pic Blanc sector** is a glacial realm of rock and ice, with the area's most exposed and challenging black pistes, including the epic Sarenne run.

The core **Alpe d'Huez sector** is characterized by enjoyable mid-altitude cruises which flow into the motorway-wide gentle superpistes, designated as beginners' zones, running down to the resort's two big base areas.

The **Signal sector** is a distinct hill in the main Alpe d'Huez area, directly accessible from town and linked to Villard-Reculas. These good cruising slopes are home to the resort's competition and floodlit night-skiing stadiums.

The **Vaujany/Oz sector** provides long, sheltered trails down to the villages for competent novices and good intermediates. This sector also contains the further satellite area of Montfrais at 1650 m (5412 ft), a compact cluster of lifts and pistes that acts as the core ski area for the village of Vaujany.

Overall, this is a big ski domain that is ideal for beginners and flattering for nervous novices, yet challenging and interesting enough for good intermediates and those of advanced abilities. Combine this with the favourable weather record, and Alpe d'Huez shines as one of the Alps' best all-round resorts.

FURTHER INFORMATION
Alpe d'Huez tourist office: current information and an excellent resort guide Ⓦ www.alpedhuez.com

COMING & GOING

Alpe d'Huez and its surrounding villages all lie close to the compact capital of the Oisans region, le Bourg-d'Oisans. The only access route in winter is the main N91 road along the Romanche Valley between Grenoble and Briançon, although the route from Briançon crosses the high-altitude and frequently snowbound Col du Lautaret near la Grave.

Daily coach transfers are available from central Grenoble and regularly from most of the closest international airports. For further details go to Ⓦ www.vfd.fr

Of course, you could always fly straight in to the town's pisted 'altiport' airstrip and heliport at les Bergers.

Altiport ❶ +33 (0)4 76 11 21 73 SAF Helicopters ❶ +33 (0)4 76 80 65 49

By road: from Grenoble, take the A480 autoroute south, straight through the city, and leave at exit number eight – signed 'Vizille-Oisans resorts' on the N91. The N91 bypasses the town of Vizille and continues towards le Bourg-d'Oisans. Some 25 km (15½ miles) after Vizille, you come to the hamlet of Rochetaillée.

For **Villard-Reculas**, **Oz-en-Oisans** and **Vaujany**, turn off to the left on to the D44 towards Allemont for the short drive up to each of these satellite stations. **Villard-Reculas** is reached via the first turn to the right (the D44b); **Oz-en-Oisans** via the second turn off to the right (the D44a), at the half-way point on the road skirting the Lac du Verney reservoir; and finally **Vaujany** via the third turn off to the right (the D43a) at the far side of the reservoir.

For **Alpe d'Huez** and **Auris**, keep straight on the N91 through Rochetaillée, bearing right, for a further 7 km (4½ miles) towards le Bourg-d'Oisans. Once at le Bourg-d'Oisans, continue straight though the town on the N91.

The turn-off for **Alpe d'Huez** (on to the D211) is well signed to the left at the first major junction, just 1.2 km (³/₄ mile) beyond le Bourg-d'Oisans. The road then climbs the famous 21 hairpin bends for the final 12 km (7¹/₂ miles) up to the resort, passing the village of Huez after 9.5 km (6 miles).

Just above Huez there are two choices, depending on which area of Alpe d'Huez you are staying in: at the junction, beside the tourist information cabin, take the turn to the right (signed 'Entrée EST') to reach the eastern quarters of town around les Bergers and l'Eclose Est; or continue straight on for all other quarters.

For **Auris**, continue on the N91 past the turn-off for Alpe d'Huez, following the signs for Briançon and Les Deux Alpes. The left-hand turn-off for Auris (on to the D211a) is a further 11.5 km (7 miles) along this main road, passing through the village of Auris to reach the ski-area base station.

ⓘ Please note that it is obligatory to carry snowchains on all of these approach roads (except the autoroute).

DISTANCES TO ALPE D'HUEZ

• Le Bourg-d'Oisans to Alpe d'Huez	13 km (8 miles)
• Grenoble to Alpe d'Huez	63 km (39¹/₂ miles)
• Chambéry to Alpe d'Huez	140 km (88 miles)
• Lyon to Alpe d'Huez	163 km (101 miles)
• Geneva to Alpe d'Huez	220 km (136¹/₂ miles)

◉ *Huez village, towards le Bourg-d'Oisans*

Parking: to deal with the massive influx of winter visitors, Alpe d'Huez and its satellite stations have provided free-of-charge open car parks and pay-to-use covered car parks at various locations around the resorts, generally beside the main lifts bases (for Alpe d'Huez, see town plans on pages 65 and 67). The covered car parks in Vaujany are free-of-charge.

ALPE D'HUEZ (VIEIL ALPE/COGNET) TOWN PLAN

KEY

i	Central tourist office	⊠	Post office
	Bucket lift		Ski pass sales point
	Chair lift		Equipment hire shop
	Gondola lift	P	Parking
€	ATM cash machine		Supermarket
+	Medical centre	+	Pharmacy

HOTELS & APARTMENTS

1. Hotel le Christina
2. Hotel le Dôme
3. Hotel Belle Aurore
4. Hotel Alp Azur
5. Hotel Grandes Rousses
6. Hotel Bel Alpe
7. Hotel le Castillan
8. Hotel Vallée Blanche

RESTAURANTS

1. Le Tarburle
2. La Cordée
3. L'Authentique
4. La Pomme de Pin
5. Au P'tit Creux
6. Le Génépi

BARS & CLUBS

1. Le Sporting
2. Fun Café
3. Igloo/Tropicana
4. Smithy's
5. Freeride
6. Les Caves de l'Alpe

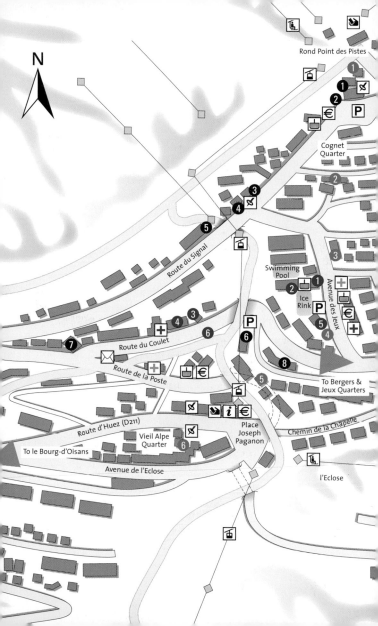

Rond Point des Pistes

Cognet Quarter

Swimming Pool

Ice Rink

Avenue des Jeux

Route du Signal

Route du Coulet

Route de la Poste

Route d'Huez (D211)

To le Bourg-d'Oisans

Vieil Alpe Quarter

Place Joseph Paganon

Chemin de la Chapelle

To Bergers & Jeux Quarters

l'Eclose

Avenue de l'Eclose

ALPE D'HUEZ (JEUX/BERGERS) TOWN PLAN

KEY

i	Information office		Ski pass sales point
	Cable car		Equipment hire shop
	Chair lift	**P**	Parking
	Gondola lift		Supermarket
€	ATM cash machine	**+**	Pharmacy
+	Medical centre	**†**	Church

HOTELS & APARTMENTS

1 Hotel Beau Soleil   **4** VVF/MMV Apartments
2 Hotel Pelvoux   **5** Hotel les Gentianes
3 Hotel l'Outa   **6** Hotel Royal Ours Blanc

RESTAURANTS

1 Chilly Powder   **4** Les Primtemps de Juliette
2 La Cordée   **5** Au Grenier
3 L'Authentique

BARS & CLUBS

1 O'Sharkeys

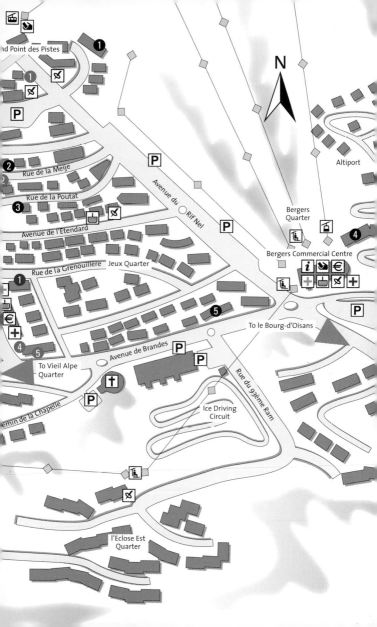

SKI AREA DATA

- Opening time · · · · · 08.45 hours
- Last lift up · · · · · 17.00 hours
- Skiable area · · · · · 10,000 hectares (24,710 acres)
- Altitude · · · · · 1120–3330 m (3675–10,926 ft)
- Vertical drop · · · · · 2210 m (7251 ft)
- Access points · · · · · 7
- Ski schools · · · · · 6

- Ski lifts · · · · · 85

Funiculars	0	Non-declutchable chair lifts	21
Cable cars	6	Declutchable chair lift	4
Gondolas	10	Button lifts	42
Inclined elevators	2		

- Capacity · · · · · 98,000 passengers/hour

- Pistes · · · · · 121 (245 km/152 miles)

Green	40	Tricks parks	2
Blue	31	Halfpipes	1
Red	33	Children's	2
Black	17	Nordic	50 km/31 miles
FIS	2		

- Hands-free ski pass · · · · · No
- Snowmaking · · · · · 770 cannons
  (covering 33 km/21 miles of pistes)
- First-aid posts · · · · · 19
- Medical centres · · · · · 3
- Mountain bars/restaurants · · · · · 16 sites
- Visitor information · · · · · www.alpedhuez.com

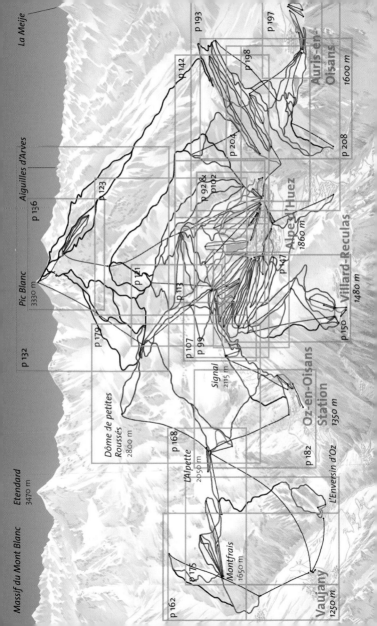

Massif du Mont Blanc

Etendard
3470 m

La Meije

Aiguilles d'Arves

Pic Blanc
3330 m

p 132

p 136

p 123

p 142

p 193

p 197

p 198

p 204

p 208

Auris-en-
Oisans
1600 m

Alpe d'Huez
1860 m

Villard-Reculas
1480 m

p 92 &
p 102

p 147

p 150

p 121

p 113

p 170

p 107

p 99

Signal
2115 m

Oz-en-Oisans
Station
1350 m

Dôme de petites
Roussés
2800 m

p 182

p 168

L'Alpette
2050 m

p 175

Montfrais
1650 m

L'Enversin d'Oz

p 162

Vaujany
1250 m

SKI PASSES

Various options are available, depending on duration and on whether you want a local or a full area pass. Prices are consistent throughout the season, with no high season supplements.

A photograph is required for all passes of more than one day's duration: the passes are not electronically readable. Lost passes will not be replaced or refunded.

All passes are available for children (5–15 years), adults (16–59 years) and seniors (60–71 years). Ski passes are free of charge for all children under 5 years of age; those for children aged 5–15 are approximately 30 per cent cheaper than adults' passes. Ski passes for guests aged 60–71 are also approximately 30 per cent cheaper than standard adults' passes; ski passes are free for visitors aged 72 and above. Various special offers and discounts are available:

Part day From first lift to 12.30 hours; from 12.30 hours to lifts' closing time, or from 15.00 hours until lifts' closing time.

Beginners A great value day pass, covering all the ski lifts and pistes within the two specially designated beginners' zones at Alpe d'Huez (marked by the green zones on the piste map), at a price approximately 60 per cent cheaper than the full area day pass. All of the satellite stations also offer special beginners' day passes for their own compact beginners' zones.

Families When a minimum of four VISALP passes are purchased at the same time, for a minimum of five days' duration and for a minimum of two adults and two children (under 20 years of age) from the same family, a 50 per cent discount is given on the fourth and subsequent ski passes.

Loyalty Returning visitors can present last year's VISALP ski pass (with a duration of five days or more) to receive a five per cent discount on a new one at the time of purchase.

Final day If you are not departing until late on your last day and wish to pack in as much skiing as possible, present your ski pass at the ski pass sales point the day after it expires to purchase a final morning or full-day extension at a much reduced rate.

🛈 Proof of age and identity is required at the time of purchase for all child, senior and family ski passes.

LOCAL SECTOR PASSES

Alpe d'Huez Covers 26 ski lifts accessing 27 pistes, including the Huez Télévillage gondola and all the lower- and mid-level ski lifts and pistes at Alpe d'Huez (excludes Marmottes gondola and all ski lifts above 2100 mid-station). Available on a daily basis only.

Auris Covers 15 ski lifts accessing 20 pistes, including all the Auris-en-Oisins and la Garde ski lifts and pistes, plus the Chalvet chair lift (and all pistes accessible from it) and return via the Alpauris chair lift from les Bergers, Alpe d'Huez. Available on a daily and weekly basis.

Oz/Vaujany Covers 21 ski lifts accessing 29 pistes, including all of the Vaujany, Montfrais, l'Alpette, Oz-en-Oisans ski lifts and pistes, all pistes linking into Alpe d'Huez, plus the Jeux button lift and the lower section of the Grandes Rousses (DMC) cable car at Alpe d'Huez. Available on a daily and weekly basis. A small optional supplement provides free access to the ice-skating rinks at both stations, plus the Vaujany swimming pool and leisure complex (before 16.00 hours and for over-18s only).

Villard-Reculas Covers eight ski lifts accessing nine pistes, including all ski lifts and pistes in Villard-Reculas, all pistes linking into Alpe d'Huez and the Grande Sure chair lift at Alpe d'Huez. Available on a daily and weekly basis.

All area ski passes are full **Grandes Rousses** passes covering all ski lifts and pistes in Alpe d'Huez, Huez, Auris-en-Oisans, Villard-Reculas, Oz-en-Oisans and Vaujany (dependent on open links). Standard area passes are available on a daily basis, or as a carnet of ten daily passes that can be used on any ten days of the season.

All Grandes Rousses passes of more than two days' duration are also designated as VISALP ski passes, which additionally include free access to a wealth of sports and leisure activities and facilities in Alpe d'Huez. These include floodlit night skiing; floodlit sledging; the ice rink; heated outdoor and indoor municipal swimming pools; the municipal sports and conference centre (see page 239 for full details of facilities); weekly classical music concert; entry to the Museum of Huez and Oisans and unlimited use of the Alpe d'Huez ski bus service.

GRANDE GALAXIE SKI REGION

All VISALP ski passes of six days' duration or more include access to all ski stations in the Grande Galaxie ski region: covering two days' skiing at Les Deux Alpes, as well as a free-of-charge day pass for Puy-St-Vincent, Serre Chevalier or the Milky Way domain straddling the French/Italian border. Visits to these stations must be made during the period of validity of your VISALP pass. Transport is not included (see page 75 for Les Deux Alpes shuttle service details).

PRICES
The longer the duration, the cheaper the equivalent daily rate. For current prices of all ski passes, tuition and childcare, please go to our website: **www.ski-ride.com**

SKI PASS SALES POINTS

You can purchase any of the full area passes offered at any of the main sales booths, which are dotted around the main resort and satellite base stations; local day passes are only available from the sales points at each respective base station.

Alpe d'Huez Grandes Rousses cable car (DMC) base station; Central Tourist Office; les Bergers commercial centre (see town plan on page 66).

Auris-en-Oisans Tourist Office – Place des Orgières.

Villard-Reculas Tourist Office – at the base of the Cloudit ski lift.

Oz-en-Oisans Poutran gondola base station.

Vaujany Cable car/gondola base station.

NORDIC SKI PASSES

Alpe d'Huez offers half-a-dozen well-maintained cross-country circuits/trails (see pages 233–5). A dedicated ski pass is available giving access to all of them, including travel on a total of 22 major ski lifts accessing most of the ski area. Passes are available on a half-day (afternoons from 12.30 hours only), full-day, weekend (any two consecutive days), week (seven days) and full-season basis. Prices are about 70 per cent less expensive than those of the standard Alpine ski passes. Week-long passes are VISAI P passes permitting free access to the full range of municipal sports and leisure activities/facilities and ski bus services in Alpe d'Huez. Cheaper local area passes are also available at each of the satellite stations, giving access to the nearest circuits only.

❶ Accident insurance is not included in basic ski pass prices, so make sure you are adequately covered and never travel without comprehensive winter sports travel insurance (see page 54).

SKI BUS

There are four lines operated by the ski bus (*navette*) service in Alpe d'Huez, all colour-coded specific to the areas they serve:

⊕ **Red Line** (Circuit Rouge): running from/to the ice rink (on avenue des Jeux), in a circuit via the Rond Point de l'Europe near les Bergers and the Rond Point de Pistes; approximately every 15 minutes from 08.50–17.45 hours.

⊕ **Orange Line** (Circuit Orange): running from/to l'Eclose via the Rond Point des Pistes >> les Bergers >> the Altiport >> Club Med and the Palais des Sports; approximately every 20 minutes from 08.55–17.45 hours.

⊕ **Green Line** (Circuit Vert): running in a circuit around the whole resort (except les Bergers) from/to Huez village: approximately every 50 minutes from 07.35–19.00 hours.

⊕ **Blue Line** (Circuit Bleu): running from/to Huez village in a circuit of the entire resort of Alpe d'Huez; every 20 minutes non-stop from 08.20–17.40 hours and approximately once per hour from 18.15–23.45 hours.

All services operate from the third week in December to the end of April. Additionally, an early season Yellow Line (Circuit Jaune) service operates from early December until the first day of operation of the four main services, running to a reduced timetable but mirroring the standard blue line service.

All services are free of charge for all visitors – no ski pass is required to use them.

Vaujany also has its own free ski bus service which serves the core village from 08.50–21.00 hours; there are also two departures per day from/to the hamlets of la Villette and le Petit Vaujany. Additionally, there is a free bus service to/from Bourg-en-Oisans via Allemont, which operates up to three times per day.

Oz-en-Oisans has a limited free shuttle service which runs three or four times every morning and afternoon, linking Oz station with Allemont and Rochetaillée.

All of the other satellite stations are quite compact, with all accommodation within strolling distance of the ski lifts and pistes, obviating the need for ski bus services.

LES DEUX ALPES SHUTTLE

Since all VISALP ski passes of minimum six days' duration include two days' skiing at nearby Les Deux Alpes, a special shuttle bus service operates from Alpe d'Huez twice per week (currently Wednesday and Thursday). The service runs from/to the VFD travel agency office at avenue de l'Eclose, in the lower Vieil Alpe quarter, and from in front of the Palais du Sports on avenue de Brandes. The bus currently departs from Alpe d'Huez at 08.30 hours, arriving in Les Deux Alpes at around 09.45 hours, leaving Les Deux Alpes for the return journey at 17.20 hours and arriving back at Alpe d'Huez at around 18.45 hours. The service operates from the last week in December to the last week in April, subject to road conditions and demand; ticket prices are excellent value, currently in single figures covering the two-way trip.

Places are limited and must be booked 48 hours in advance: bookings may be made directly at the main VFD office or at their branch desk at the Palais du Sports.

VFD central booking: ☏ +33 (0)4 76 80 31 60

EQUIPMENT

Most visitors travelling with a tour operator tend to leave the organization of equipment to their reps; newly arrived guests will then usually be taken en masse for gear fitting on their first morning before going on the mountain. Virtually every sports shop in Alpe d'Huez and the surrounding satellite stations offers a snowsports equipment rental operation, so there is plenty of choice, and competition to keep standards high and prices keen. All of the major franchises are represented, including Sport2000 and Twinner, InterSport and SkiSet, and there are a number of independent businesses providing bespoke services, including latest models hire and delivery/pick-up to/from your accommodation.

TUITION

The French National Ski School – **l'École du Ski Français** (ESF) – has a number of offices in Alpe d'Huez serving all quarters of the resort, as well as in all of the satellite stations. Alpe d'Huez is also served by the International Ski School, **École de Ski Internationale** (ESI).

Everything from standard group lessons for absolute beginners and progressing novices up to advanced one-to-one teaching clinics for expert all-mountain riders is available, both for ski and snowboard. Children's classes are available with or without lunch at most sites; please enquire locally. Minimum ages acceptable vary from village to village; details are given alongside the following contact details for each station.

The ESF also offer cross-country skiing, Telemark and competition training courses. Additionally, they offer Ski Évolutif lessons, as pioneered at les Arcs, where participants begin learning on very short skis before progressing to standard-sized models, a method which many beginners find easier to master.

Alpe d'Huez The main piste-side **ESF** offices and meeting points are based at the Rond Point des Pistes area, in the wooden chalet just in front of the Grandes Rousses (DMC) cable car base station, and at the rear entrance to the Bergers commercial centre in les Bergers. The central sales and information office is based at the central tourist office, beside the Télécentre bucket lift base station. Additionally, there are branch offices at avenue des Jeux, next to the Hotel les Primtemps de Juillette; and at the commercial centre in l'Eclose Est quarter. Children are accepted from 4 years of age. Central information office ☎ +33 (0)4 76 80 94 23 ⓦ www.esf-alpedhuez.com

The **ESI** piste-side offices and meeting points are also at the Rond Point des Pistes and les Bergers areas, in wooden chalet cabins at the bases of the pistes. The central information and sales office is based on the route du Signal, at the MGM rental shop under the Hotel Alp Azur. ☎ +33 (0)4 76 80 42 77 ⓦ www.ecoledeskiinternationale.com

For more experienced visitors, the **Alpe d'Huez Bureau des Guides** is also a good option. The team of high mountain guides is, unlike standard ski instructors, qualified to guide on the high-altitude off-piste glacier routes. The guides also offer heli-skiing, ice climbing, Via Ferrata rock climbing and ski touring to other regional ski stations. The central information and booking office is based at the ESF chalet at the Rond Point des Pistes, near the Grandes Rousses (DMC) cable car base station. ☎ +33 (0)4 76 80 42 55

Villard-Reculas The ESF office is at the tourist office, near the base of the Cloudit ski lift; meeting points are at the base of the lift. Children are accepted from 4 years of age. ☎ +33 (0)4 76 80 40 01

Auris-en-Oisans The ESF office is at the tourist office, at the base station commercial centre in place des Orgières; the meeting points are by the Sures chair lift. Children are accepted from 3 years of age. ☎ +33 (0)4 76 80 15 25 ⊕ www.aurisesf.com

Oz-en-Oisans The ESF office faces the Résidence les Myrtilles, near l'Alpette gondola base station, as do the meeting points. Children are accepted from 4 years of age. ☎ +33 (0)4 76 80 74 93 ⊕ www.esf-ozenoisans.com

Vaujany The ESF office is at the cable car/gondolas base station in the lower village centre, as are the meeting points. Children are accepted from 4–13 years of age (over 13s join the standard ski school classes). ☎ +33 (0)4 76 80 71 80 ⊕ www.esf-vaujany.com

Vaujany also has a couple of independent tuition options, offering bespoke services for individuals, families and small groups: Massif – high mountain guiding, off-piste skiing, ice climbing and heli-skiing. ☎ +33 (0)6 07 97 38 11

Christelle – all levels, plus off-piste initiation. ☎ +33 (0)6 83 14 05 74

▲ *Welcome to the wonderful world of snowsports*

CHILDCARE & SNOW GARDENS

There are gentle, fenced-off Snow Gardens especially for children available at all stations. The most extensive are those at Alpe d'Huez, which has two of the best in the Alps. All the sites are controlled by the ESF, which has specialist nursery ski instructors available to introduce children aged over 4 (3 years 9 months accepted at Auris) to the world of snowsports; child/beginners' lift passes are required to use these facilities, but these are free for all children under 5 years of age. Various options are bookable via the ski schools at each station, including half days, full days and weekly, with or without lunch included.

Additionally, all the ski schools offer standard skiing lessons in each sector's main beginners' areas for children over 5 years of age; prices are generally around 10 per cent cheaper than those of adult classes.

Alpe d'Huez The main children's Snow Gardens are situated at the base of the Jeux button lift at the Rond Point des Pistes area and by the Poussins button lifts at les Bergers base area. These extensive areas are equipped with simple-to-use magic carpet conveyors and/or rope tows, colourful obstacles, cartoon statues and exciting igloo tunnels.

VACCINATIONS

Resort childcare services may ask for proof that your child has had certain vaccinations. You are advised to contact them well in advance of your trip to ascertain exact requirements.

The ESI also operates its own smaller Snow Garden at the Rond Point des Pistes area at Alpe d'Huez for children 2½–4 years of age and includes free equipment hire. This service is bookable for five days' duration, but is only available from 10.00–noon.

Les Eterlous The ESF's dedicated crèche for children 2½–5 years of age is located in les Bergers, just behind the Résidence le Christiania. The crèche is well equipped and has its own little Snow Garden. The service must be booked in advance and is available on a half-day, full-day or weekly basis; meals can also be provided. Children are supervised by a team of qualified nursery instructors to take part in a variety of indoor/outdoor leisure and learning activities and can participate in basic skiing lessons in the Snow Garden (equipment hire is not included).
🕻 +33 (0)4 76 80 31 69 🌐 www.esf-alpedhuez.com

Les Crapouilloux Alpe d'Huez's central crèche, for children 2–10 years of age, located in the place Joseph Paganon in the centre of the Vieil Alpe quarter, not far from the tourist office. Children are

---

PREPARATION

Since most childcare services in the resorts include outdoor activities, ensure that your children are prepared: they should have warm clothing, gloves, proper sunglasses or goggles, and handkerchiefs, and should use sun-protection lotion. Helmets are strongly recommended.

It is also a good idea to pack some snacks for them and to put your contact details in their pockets.

supervised by a qualified nursery team. The crèche is well equipped and has a ball pit and video games. Indoor and outdoor activities are arranged and the service can be coordinated with ski lessons with the ESF, including transport to and from the ski school. Bookable for four, six or eight hours per day, with or without meals included. A useful lunchtime only service is also available to collect your children from ski school, take them to the crèche for lunch, then return them to ski school afterwards. ☎ +33 (0)4 76 11 39 23

Villard-Reculas The Snow Garden is right next to the ESF office (see page 77 for ESF location and contact details). Children are accepted from 4 years of age.

Auris-en-Oisans The children's club 'les Marmottes' accepts children aged 18 months–10 years and operates at the Snow Garden beside place des Écrins, in the upper part of the base station. The service is available from 09.00–17.00 hours and is bookable by the hour, half day or full day, with special rates for three- or six-day packages; lunch can also be arranged. ☎ +33 (0)4 76 80 08 36

Oz-en-Oisans The ESF operate a Snow Garden at the beginners' slopes area; children are accepted from the ages of 4–6 years (see page 78 for ESF contact details). The village also has a crèche service, called Halte-Garderie, based at Résidence les Airelles near l'Alpette gondola. The crèche is open from 09.00–17.00 hours and accepts children aged 6 months–6 years. The service is bookable by the hour, half day or full day, with special rates for six-day packages; the crèche can also coordinate its services with those of the ESF, as per above. ☎ +33 (0)4 76 80 75 06

Vaujany The ESF Snow Garden is located at the Montfrais area at the top of the Vaujany-Villette/Villette-Montfrais gondola; the service is available for children over the age of 4 (see page 78 for ESF contact details). The village has two crèche options, as follows:

The purpose-built nursery is located at the end of the lower village centre, just above the road nearest to the line of the Vaujany-Villette gondola. Children aged 6 months–5 years are accepted, and the crèche is open from 09.00–18.00 hours; the service must be booked in advance and is available on an hourly, half-day and full-day basis, with or without lunch. Services can be coordinated with ski school. ☎ +33 (0)4 76 80 77 53

The village's leisure centre, located below the lower village and reachable via an inclined elevator from the lifts' base station, has a team of qualified childcare staff to care for children aged 6–11 years and to guide them for the sports facilities on-site, and in outdoor activities such as sledding and ice skating. The centre is open from 10.30–20.00 hours, and the childcare service is bookable on an hourly or daily basis. ☎ +33 (0)4 76 79 83 83

NON-SKIERS

Alpe d'Huez is one of the best resorts in the Alps for non-skiers, with a wealth of sports and leisure activities and facilities on offer and an extensive network of prepared walking/snowshoe trails throughout and alongside the ski area, allowing non-skiers to access most high-altitude restaurants and viewpoints. Pedestrian passes are the same as the cross-country ski passes and permit travel on no less than 22 ski lifts, including all major gondolas and cable cars, plus some chair lifts from and to the satellite stations. A dedicated walkers' lift map is published and is available from all tourist offices and ski pass sales points.

SERVICES

Medical Centres There are well-equipped trauma and X-ray suites available at three separate medical centres in Alpe d'Huez: one in the town centre on avenue des Jeux; one on the route du Signal, just next to the Schuss button lift and directly accessible from the pistes; and one at les Bergers commercial centre, again easily accessible from the pistes (see town plans on pages 65 and 67). There are 19 first-aid posts throughout the ski area, with piste-patrol staff in attendance every day during lift opening hours; in the event of a major accident, casualties will be brought to Alpe d'Huez or evacuated to the nearest appropriate facilities.

Groupe Médical de la Meije ⓐ route du Signal ⓣ +33 (0)4 76 80 37 30
Centre Médical des Bergers ⓐ les Bergers commercial centre
ⓣ +33 (0)4 76 80 69 29
Groupe Médical ⓐ avenue des Jeux ⓣ +33 (0)4 76 80 35 84

The medical staff will contact your insurance company, although you will have to pay any initial costs, excluded by any excess clauses, on-site. Make sure that your insurance covers heli-rescue, piste rescue and ambulance transport, as well as medical and hospital expenses.
ⓘ Always carry ID and your insurance details. It is also advisable to carry a small first-aid kit for dealing with minor cuts and bruises (see Health & Safety, pages 49–54).

Telephones Phonecard and coin-operated public telephone booths are plentiful within the Alpe d'Huez town itself, and there is at least one cluster of booths at each satellite base station. GSM mobile phone coverage is virtually 100 per cent.

WCs In the Alpe d'Huez sectors, public toilets are located at the Bergers commercial centre, all stations of the Grandes Rousses (DMC) cable car, and at the top station of the Marmottes III cable car.

In Villard, there are WCs beside the tourist office at the base of the Cloudit ski lift, as well as in the village centre. In Oz, WCs are located at the Poutran I gondola base station. In Vaujany, there are WCs at the Espace Patrimoine cultural centre in the centre of the lower village, at the top of the escalators from the lifts' base station. All of the larger mountain restaurants also have public toilets.

ATMs Cash machines are dotted around Alpe d'Huez town; the closest to the slopes is at the Bergers commercial centre (see town plans on pages 65 and 67). There is also an ATM in Vaujany, located at the end of the buildings on the road immediately above the lifts' base station, nearest to and parallel with the line of the Vaujany-Villette gondola.

Mountain restaurants There are 16 different sites in the ski area which are directly accessible by piste; all offer a full bar service and most have snack food and self-service fare in canteen-style surroundings. Around half of these also have good à la carte options, offering more refined gastronomic menus and ambiance; reservations are required at busy periods.

There is also a choice of venues at Auris, Villard and Vaujany base areas, easily accessible from the pistes and/or lift bases.

➔ *See pages 221–32 for specific restaurant reviews.*

▶ *Marmottes restaurant, Alpe d'Huez*

SNOWFALL HISTORY & ANALYSIS

Although precipitation is unpredictable at very long range, patterns do emerge that are observable over a number of seasons. Using this data, you can tell if your preferred period of travel has historically seen good snow cover. The magic figure is 100 cm (39 in) – once snow depth exceeds this mark, conditions are generally good throughout the ski area and will remain so for a more extended period.

Despite its southern latitude, the Grandes Rousses domain has a good percentage of high-altitude, snow-sure pistes. The Glacier de Sarenne and the uppermost pistes in the Pic Blanc sector secure an ealy start to the season and ensure that late season visitors will not be disappointed. All base areas and satellite station links are covered by an extensive network of snowmaking equipment. The only negative issue is that lower slopes can become very heavy and slushy in warm weather.

The chart below details combined averages recorded over three seasons immediately before the publication of this guide. Visit **www.ski-ride.com** for live snow reports.

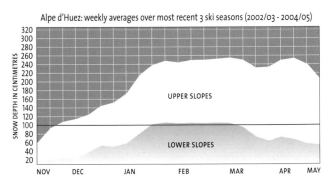

Alpe d'Huez: weekly averages over most recent 3 ski seasons (2002/03 - 2004/05)

PREVIOUS SEASONS' SNOWFALL BREAKDOWN BY YEAR

The following charts detail the snowfall history for the three most recent seasons. Data from these charts was used to compile the combined averages chart on the preceding page.

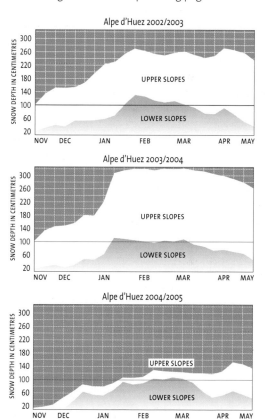

ALPE D'HUEZ BASE

The resort of Alpe d'Huez sprawls over the mountainside and is divided into distinct quarters; where you stay affects where and how you access the pistes and lifts. There are three principal base areas: the Rond Point des Pistes area at the uppermost point of the main resort, serving the Cognet and Vieil Alpe quarters; the Bergers area at the main open car parks and commercial centre at les Bergers, serving the Jeux and Bergers quarters; and l'Eclose Est area extending from the central place Joseph Paganon to the church. This area is the arrival point for the Huez village gondola lift (Télévillage) and serves the lower part of the Vieil Alpe quarter as well as l'Eclose Est quarter itself.

FIRST ACCESS – ROND POINT DES PISTES

The Vieil Alpe quarter is the heart of the original village, centred around the place Joseph Paganon just below the central tourist office. The main road snakes through town via a short tunnel just above this central square. The buildings in this quarter are perched in terrace formation on the hillside, with terrific views over the deep valley to the peaks in the Ecrins National Park opposite. A two-way open gondola, known as a bucket lift and named the Télécentre, rises from its base station next to the central tourist office, passing via a mid-station on the route du Signal in the upper part of town, to provide transport to and from the busy Rond Point des Pistes base area. The Télécentre's upper station is right next to the Signal sector's main lifts, just a short stroll from the Grandes Rousses (DMC) cable car and the principal beginners' zone.

◀ *Télécentre bucket lift in central Alpe d'Huez*

The parallel Signal chair lift and triple button lifts (a fast declutchable chair lift will replace these in 2007), and the Stade button lift, serve the Alpe d'Huez side of the Signal sector; all except the Stade lift reach the summit of the Signal and so provide a link to the pistes towards Villard-Reculas.

The Grandes Rousses (DMC) cable car provides the principal uplift to the core Alpe d'Huez ski area plus onward connections to Oz-en-Oisans, Vaujany and the glacial zone on Pic Blanc. The entire lower central slopes area to the left of the cable car base station is designated as the principal beginners' zone and is served by a mass of button lifts; the Town sector slopes flow gently through this zone to make home runs back to the base station and resort. A number of snack bar/restaurants are accessible from the pistes, as is the top end of the avenue du Rif Nel, which has further bars and restaurants and equipment hire shops.

From the Rond Point des Pistes area, pisted tracks lead around the periphery of the resort to allow on-piste access back to the various quarters of town. The track running along the base of the Signal sector slopes, parallel to the line of the bucket lift, branches off via a pisted tunnel under the route du Signal road, close to the short Schuss button lift, emerging beside the Télécentre mid-station to continue down through the centre of the village. It uses pisted footbridges over the roads to provide an on-piste link through town to the Télécentre base station/central tourist office, and continues above the central place Joseph Paganon to link with l'Eclose Est slopes and lifts.

The Grande Sure chair lift, serving the Signal sector and linking towards Villard-Reculas, departs from the far side of the Vieil Alpe quarter, and can be reached via a pisted track starting from opposite the post office on the route de la Poste. The Signal sector's Petit Sure red piste descends to the base of this chair lift, and the link track which flows around the periphery of town can also be used to get here. This link track continues descending right down to Huez village, corresponding with the Village blue piste towards the Télévillage gondola lift base station.

TÉLÉCENTRE BUCKET LIFT

  10½ mins ▲▼
- 45 m (148 ft) vertical rise
- 771 m (705 yd) long

The mid-station is 3½ minutes from the base station, 7 minutes from the upper station.

An unusual lift and an interesting piece of engineering, travelling through the middle of Alpe d'Huez from/to the central tourist office to/from the Rond Point des Pistes area, via a mid-station at the route du Signal, to save walking in this hilly part of the resort. The open lift cages are arranged in clusters of six, and the lift mechanism runs with a stop-and-start motion to accommodate each cluster as it passes through the stations. The winding journey gives good views across the resort, over the open-air swimming pool and ice rink towards the peaks beyond.

On arrival at the Rond Point des Pistes area, dismount on to the arrival platform and exit via the short steps directly ahead on to the green-graded link-track piste. The parallel Signal triple button lift and chair lift are first left; the Grandes Rousses (DMC) gondola and main Rond Point des Pistes area are a short walk ahead.

If you are descending via the Télécentre, you can dismount at either of the lower stations to access their respective levels of the resorts.

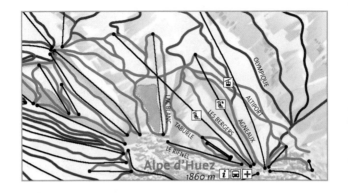

FIRST ACCESS – BERGERS

The Jeux and Bergers quarters are expansions of the original village and extend from the central avenue des Jeux across to the Altiport airstrip. These quarters of the resort are much flatter than the older part of the village, with long, straight avenues running across the Jeux quarter to the arterial avenue du Rif Nel and the Bergers quarter. The Bergers area has an easily accessible lifts' base and extensive beginners' zone, with home-run pistes running down to a busy commercial centre by the main roadside. Those staying in the Vieil Alpe or l'Eclose Est quarters, or in Huez village, can use the cross-town Bergers chair lift to reach this area.

The double Rifnel button lifts rise parallel to the avenue du Rif Nel, making a connection up to the Rond Point des Pistes area, with a green piste, also called the Rifnel, running down parallel to the lift-line to provide an on-piste link in the opposite direction. A cluster of button lifts (the 'Poussins') serves the lowest level beginners' slopes; the principal beginners' slopes directly above the base area are served by the centrally located declutchable six-seater Romains chair lift. The attractive chalet suburb above the Altiport area has pisted tracks linking to and from the main lower slopes and is also served by this main chair lift.

Another chair lift (the Fontbelle) provides a cross-mountain link in the direction of the 2100 area interchange, but the principal lift out of the Bergers base area is the Marmottes 1 gondola, located immediately behind the commercial centre and linking directly with the Plat des Marmottes level at 2300 m (7544 ft). The two-way Alpauris chair lift also departs and arrives at the far side of the commercial centre, linking to and from the Auris sector.

The whole Bergers base area buzzes with activity and is popular with non-skiers too, drawn here by the commercial centre and the designated sledging piste next to it. There are just a couple of piste-side terrace bar/restaurants but there are plenty more inside the animated commercial centre, which is directly accessible from the pistes.

▲ *Bergers base area and the lower flanks of Pic Blanc*

L'ECLOSE SLOPES

Although accessible to all slope users, the compact l'Eclose Est hill-side is also designated as a sledging area and is floodlit a couple of evenings a week (see page 240). The slopes can be reached on foot from the place Joseph Paganon or the chemin de la Chapelle; access is also easy from and to the resort's l'Eclose Est quarter, at the top of the lifts beside the small l'Eclose commercial centre.

The Eclose chair lift serves this hillside and links with the two-way Bergers chair lift, an almost horizontal cross-town link to and from the Bergers base area. There is also a button lift serving these slopes, rising up parallel to the right of the Eclose chair lift; although this is tucked quietly away at the margins of the resort it is a very noteworthy installation, as it marks the site of the world's very first declutching drag lift, inaugurated in 1936 by Jean Pomagalski, founder of the Poma ski-lift company.

This area is also the arrival and departure point for the two-way Télévillage gondola lift serving Huez village; its upper station is just beside the base of the Eclose chair lift. The pisted link track that flows through the Vieil Alpe quarter also passes through here to complete an on-piste link to Huez, corresponding to the red Huez piste. There are a few piste-side snack bar/restaurants with terraces around the base slopes, mostly all at small hotels that skirt this area.

🔺 *L'Eclose hillside, designated as a sledging area*

ECLOSE CHAIR LIFT

5 mins ▲▼

- 61 m (200 ft) vertical rise
- 2400 passengers/hour

Slow old chair serving the Eclose green pistes/sledging slopes and providing an easy link with the Bergers chair lift towards the Bergers base area. On arrival at the top, the pistes begin immediately to the left and right. The Bergers chair lift is a short skate ahead left and l'Eclose Est quarter a short walk/skate over to the far right.

BERGERS CHAIR LIFT

8 mins ▲▼

- 16 m (52 ft) vertical rise
- 637 m (697 yd) long
- 2400 passengers/hour

An almost horizontal cross-town link connecting l'Eclose Est with Bergers. The journey passes over the Circuit de l'Oisans ice-driving circuit and central piste-basher garages, giving a good view over all quarters of the resort to aid orientation.

At l'Eclose Est, the lift is a short, flat skate from the top of the Eclose chair lift, which arrives just next to it; this area is also just a short walk from l'Eclose Est quarter itself. If you are travelling from Bergers, you can either skate over to the roadside and to the rear of the small commercial centre at l'Eclose Est quarter, or access the Vieil Alpe quarter using the green-graded Eclose pistes.

At the Bergers end, the lift arrives and departs next to the Tremplin restaurant at the side of the commercial centre. The Fontbelle chair lift and twin Poussins button lifts are a short inclined skate ahead left; the Marmottes 1 gondola and Alpauris chair lift are to the far side of the commercial centre.

HUEZ

This is simply a home-run link piste down to Huez village, running from the base of the l'Eclose hillside down parallel to the line of the Télévillage gondola lift. There's nothing really exciting about this route, but it does have the novelty value of running down lower than the road-climb up to Alpe d'Huez. The route affords great views over Huez and the valley below, towards the beautiful peaks of the Chaine de Belledonne and the Ecrins National Park on the horizon ahead. The piste eventually swoops through a short tunnel to cross under the road before merging with the similar profile Village blue piste towards the base of Huez's Télévillage gondola lift.

VILLAGE

Beginning as the green-graded link track which runs along the base of the Signal slopes, this piste skirts the Vieil Alpe quarter of Alpe d'Huez to provide an on-piste link down to Huez village. Once at the far side of the resort, the route meets and crosses the Petite Sure red piste and crosses under the line of the Grande Sure chair lift (join the Petite Sure piste to link with this lift below left). Past this point, you are joined by the Coqs red piste from above right, continuing as an easy, if often slushy, winding cruise close to Alpe d'Huez's D211 approach road. The similar profile Huez red variation emerges from a short tunnel under the road to the left, and the Village blue continues the final descent towards Huez. Approaching the village, the piste veers left towards the base of the Télévillage gondola lift. There is a small rustic bar/restaurant (Le Savoyard) on the left, just above the lift station. Huez village centre is just a short stroll along the road to the left.

TÉLÉVILLAGE GONDOLA LIFT

 9 mins ▲▼

- 298 m (978 ft) vertical rise
- 1135 m (1242 yd) long
- 500 passengers/hour

An old-fashioned 'bubble' gondola which connects Huez village to Alpe d'Huez. It operates on the Pulse system (alternately speeding up and slowing down) to allow its five-cabin clusters to pass through the lower and upper stations. There is an underground car park (and public WCs) beside the base station, located a short stroll from the heart of the village. The lift platform is reached by a flight of stairs up from the roadside; go to the left-hand side of the platform to board the lift. The tiny, bubble-shaped cabins are very cramped and are really only suitable for a maximum of two passengers; as the automatic doors are a bit stiff, assistance is often required from the operator. The external gear-holders are also quite small and don't accommodate wide-tipped skis. Poles should be carried inside.

The journey up crosses over the D211 approach road to/from Alpe d'Huez, eventually arriving a few metres from the Eclose chair lift. For onward links, either take the Eclose chair lift to link with the Bergers chair lift towards the Bergers base area, or stroll over the pisted bridge ahead left, above the place Joseph Paganon, to reach the Télécentre bucket lift.

🔺 *Télévillage gondola lift 'bubbles', rising up from Huez village*

BEGINNERS' ZONES

All the lower slopes surrounding and immediately above the Rond Point des Pistes and Bergers base areas are groomed to form motorway-wide superpistes. These are designated as huge beginners' zones and are clearly marked by green shading on the piste map; they are also signed as such on the pistes themselves, instructing all users travelling through to limit their speed.

JEUX

This is the extensive beginners' zone at the Rond Point des Pistes area, fanning out on the slopes wide to the left of the Grandes Rousses (DMC) cable car station. The sheer extent of the area and variety of pistes within it means that this zone provides the full gamut of first-week challenges for beginners.

The ESF and ESI ski schools have offices in the central base area in front of the cable car station. Their classes' meeting-point poles are on the flat snowfield behind the prominent ESF chalet and the main beginners lifts and pistes are around 250 m (274 yd) beyond these. The nearest lift suitable for beginners is the almost horizontal Grenouilles button lift, which starts at the far end of the ski school classes' meeting area and runs directly away from the Rond Point des Pistes, alongside the Nordic trail which shares this area. This lift is free to use for all responsible users and no ski pass is required; it links with the Poutran button lift to reach the Boucle de Poutran Nordic circuit and the Violettes green piste. The longer, steeper triple Jeux button lifts are the first on the right at the main beginners' slopes; these rise all the way up to the busy 2100 area interchange. The excellent, well-equipped, children's Snow Garden is at the base of the Jeux button lifts.

Complete beginners will be taken to the short twin Ecole button lifts, just past the Jeux lifts and serving the gentlest slopes out in the middle of this wide open zone. Further past these are the Babars button lifts: there are two lift lines, the shorter one on the right serves the same easy slopes as the Ecole lifts; the longer one on the left rises much higher to reach the Snow Park and La Plage des Neiges restaurant on the hillside above.

The central slopes contain a number of named pistes, all of them graded green although some are actually easy blues: the Respect and Sagnes, both running from the top of and parallel to the line of the triple Jeux button lifts; the Babars, from the top of the longest Babars lift and running down between the Ecole and Babars lifts; the Piste de Bob, again from the top of the longest Babars lift but running down the left-hand side of the Snow Park; and the Chardons, which starts from the top of the Jeux button lifts and flows out wide to the right of the Snow Park. All pistes flow back into the open flat area at the base of the beginners' zone and require a stroll to make it back to the Rond Point des Pistes.

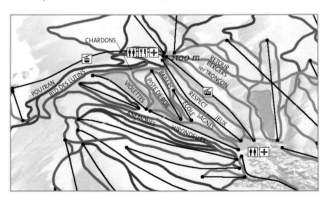

JEUX BUTTON LIFTS

6 mins

- 240 m (787 ft) vertical rise
- 1535 m (1679 yd) long
- 900 passengers/hour x 3

A set of three, parallel-running, button lifts which rise up the most central and longest slopes in the beginners' zone, shadowing the line of the Grandes Rousses (DMC) cable car to the major 2100 area interchange. Just before they arrive at the top, all three lifts rise a bit more steeply over a specially constructed bridge, built to save piste users in this busy area from having to cross the lift lines by being able to run underneath them. On arrival, U-turn to either side, clear of the parallel lifts, for all green pistes back to the resort or go straight ahead for the restaurant and cable car. More experienced visitors can also use these lifts to queue-jump the cable car base station to reach the runs towards Oz-en-Oisans.

FIRST DAY

Beginners travelling with a tour operator tend to leave the organization of equipment rental to their reps and are normally taken for equipment fitting, en masse with other newly arrived guests, early on their first morning before going on to the slopes.

If booked into ski school, they will then be advised where to meet, or accompanied to whichever beginners' rendevous area is nearest to their accommodation. Ski school generally begins around 10.00 hours.

◐ *Follow the leader... the younger you are the easier it is*

BERGERS

The entire central hillside above the base area is pisted and open, and is effectively one giant green-graded piste, although there are actually five named and way-marked routes spread out across the slopes. Looking up from the base area, these are, from left to right: the Taburle piste running down under the lower section of the Fontbelle chair lift line; les Bergers and Agneaux, flowing side-by-side down the central slopes under the main lift lines; and finally, the Altiport and Loup Blanc over to the far side of the Marmottes I gondola lift. All these pistes are practically identical – gently undulating wide runways with plenty of room for manoeuvre. They are served by the Romains 6-seater declutchable chair lift, which has a magic carpet conveyor belt to make getting on easier.

The short twin Poussins button lifts are the principal lifts for absolute beginners. They depart from just above the sledging piste at the side of the Bergers commercial centre, nearest Alpe d'Huez town. The slopes flowing down both sides of these lift lines are the gentlest in the area, and are out of the way of the main piste traffic crossing to the commercial centre and main lifts.

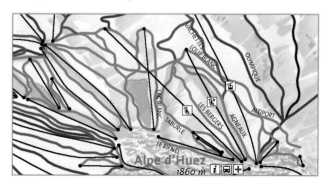

The well-laid out children's Snow Garden is immediately to the left of these Poussins lifts, safely fenced off from the busy main slopes. This facility is monitored by the ESF who, along with the ESI ski school, have an office at the Bergers commercial centre. Both ski school's classes' meeting point poles fan out in the area immediately behind the commercial centre. The centre functions as a base lodge and houses all facilities.

Over to the far left, two long button lifts, both called the Rifnel, run next to and parallel with the avenue du Rif Nel, providing a link up to the higher Rond Point des Pistes level as well as serving the long and gentle Le Rifnel green piste which flows back down to Bergers. This piste is also designated as an across-town link route for Nordic skiers.

RIFNEL BUTTON LIFTS

- 70 m (230 ft) vertical rise
- 850 m (930 yd) long
- 600 passengers/hour x 2

Twin, parallel-running button lifts which run along the side of the avenue du Rif Nel from the Bergers base area up to the upper level of town, and provide a link up to the Rond Point des Pistes base area. They also serve Le Rifnel green piste, which runs back parallel to them to make the return link to the Bergers base area. On the journey up, the lift lines bend to the right before they arrive level with the hotel Beau Soleil, a short skate from the Lac Blanc button lift serving the central Town sector slopes. Turn left and skate past the hotel to reach the Rond Point des Pistes area and the Grandes Rousses (DMC) cable car, or U-turn back down the lift line to join Le Rifnel green piste back towards Bergers.

ALPE D'HUEZ TOWN SKI SECTOR

Most of the pistes within this busy sector are big and bland, providing easy home runs back to town, However, the runs descending from the 2300 area interchange at the top of the Marmottes I gondola lift provide good warm-up runs and are fast enough to house the resort's Super Giant competition course. This sector also contains two good-sized Snow Parks.

GRANDES ROUSSES (DMC) CABLE CAR – 1er TRONÇON

- 246 m (807 ft) vertical rise
- 1484 m (1624 yd) long
- 3000 passengers/hour

When is a cable car not a cable car? When it's a giant gondola! This is the arterial lift for Alpe d'Huez's core ski area, departing from the busy Rond Point des Pistes base area in the upper part of town. The lift mechanism declutches the cabins from the haul cable and they move slowly through the station to ease getting on/off. The journey up gives a bird's eye view over virtually the entire Town sector and base areas below, arriving at the 2100 area interchange where the cabins declutch again and take a couple of minutes to pass through a mid-station to allow passengers to disembark/join at this level. Remain in the cabin if you want to continue on the second part of the journey (see page 117). If alighting al the 2100 level, leave ahead right to step out on to the start of the pistes beside the Chantebise 2100 restaurant.

❶ This lift is accessible to pedestrians but is not accessible to reduced-rate beginners' ski pass holders.

◀ *How high can you go? Big air in the Alpe d'Huez Snow Park*

2100 AREA INTERCHANGE

This is the busiest lift and pistes' interchange in the Grandes Rousses domain, spread over the wide Lac Besson plateau at 2100 m (6888 ft) directly above Alpe d'Huez. The main focal point is the Grandes Rousses (DMC) cable car mid-station and the adjacent Chantebise 2100 terrace restaurant (see page 222). Being able to join the cable car at this level saves having to return to the base station, a boon when conditions start to get slushy on the lower slopes. The station building houses WCs and a piste patrol information/first-aid point. Right next door is the big and buzzing Chantebise 2100 restaurant, its huge split level terraces overlooking the pistes that flow into and through this busy confluence area. There is a snack kiosk by the main entrance to the terrace, nearest the cable car station, and plenty of gear racks in the surrounding access area (the small 'jeton' vending machine at the snack kiosk issues tokens to operate the lockable racks). A large piste map and information board is located at the entrance/exit to the lift station.

The Poutran gondola lift (see page 186) also arrives at this altitude, coming from the small satellite resort of Oz-en-Oisans. Its upper station is tucked behind that of the cable car, a short stroll from the busy main plateau. Three parallel-running button lifts (the Jeux lifts) arrive at this same town-side of the buildings, having journeyed up from the Rond Point des Pistes base area. A little tunnel underneath the final section of these lifts allows piste traffic to flow unimpeded to the top of the Jeux beginners' zone and the Poutran red and Boulevard des Lutins blue routes towards Oz-en-Oisans, which begin on the far side of the lift lines. This direction also takes you towards La Plage des Neiges mountain bar/restaurant (see page 223) and this sector's biggest Snow Park.

The frozen lake flats beyond the Chantebise 2100 restaurant are home to the Boucle des Lacs Nordic circuit and pedestrian trail, intertwined with a snowmobile circuit. The lovely Chalet du Lac Besson mountain restaurant (see page 223) is on the quieter far side of this area, reached via the Nordic and walking routes.

A couple of hundred metres in front of the main station buildings is the get-on area for the Lievre Blanc chair lift, providing secondary uplift into the core Alpe d'Huez Mid Sector, the pistes of which are visible on the flanks of Pic Blanc above, flowing back into and through this plateau. The onward main route towards Alpe d'Huez directly below is called the 1er Tronçon and is graded green. It is a runway-wide gentle blue-equivalent cruise on the edges of the Jeux beginners' zone, with prominent piste markings informing piste users that excessive speed is prohibited. The 1er Tronçon heads directly down the line of the Grandes Rousses (DMC) cable car and provides an easy home-run cruise down to the Rond Point des Pistes base area at the foot of the cable car. The compact hillside ahead right above the town is the Signal de la Grande Sure in the Signal/Villard Sector (see page 145).

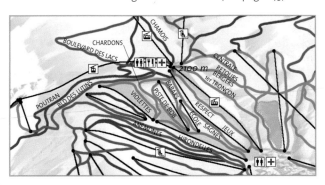

ALPE D'HUEZ / GRANDES ROUSSES

RETOUR BERGERS

This is a way-marked route which traverses diagonally all the way across the slopes above town, connecting the 2100 area level with the lower Bergers area slopes. The route crosses the line of the Lac Blanc button lift halfway down; other than that this handy link holds no surprises and delivers you over on to the wide superpistes above the Bergers base area.

LAC BLANC BUTTON LIFT

6 mins	• 245 m (804 ft) vertical rise • 1500 m (1641 yd) long • 900 passengers/hour

Serving the secondary Snow Park immediately above town and handy for gaining height from this end of town, this lift saves a walk to the other lifts first thing in the morning. The lift departs from close to the hotel Beau Soleil and the arrival point of the Rifnel button lift linking up from the Bergers base area. Beware when mounting the lift as there can be a violent jolt as the declutchable lift poles reconnect with the haul cable. The journey up skirts the edge of the Snow Park, which is to your left, giving you a good opportunity to check out its modules and plan your attack. The lift track is crossed by traffic on the green Retour Bergers link piste, coming from the left; traffic should be looking out for you, but stay alert. There is then a steep final section before the dismount level. On arrival, turn left to go towards the Snow Park or turn right for either the Lac Blanc green run parallel down the lift line or to head towards the Bergers area via the adjoining Vachettes blue piste. ❶ Caution – fast traffic coming round the bend from above left.

FONTBELLE CHAIR LIFT

14 mins	• 331 m (1086 ft) vertical rise • 1746 m (1910 yd) long • 2174 passengers/hour

A painfully slow link-lift out of the main Bergers base area that is worth taking on good weather days, especially if there are big queues for the Marmottes I gondola lift, because of the amount of ground it covers and the link it provides towards the major 2100 area interchange. The lift base is centrally located at the Bergers base area and has a magic carpet conveyor at the get-on point. The lift crosses the lower ski area diagonally, mirroring the route of the green Retour Bergers route travelling on the ground below in the opposite direction.

On arrival, turn right to start the Fontbelle green link piste down to join the Retour Bergers route or to access the Snow Park, or turn left to head towards the 2100 area interchange. The mid-station for the Grandes Rousses (DMC) cable car is visible ahead. This direction also allows you to U-turn down to the left to take the Centrale green piste towards the Snow Park.

The link track towards the 2100 area interchange is quite gentle and often requires a skate, but it works fine and links best with the nearby Lièvre Blanc chair lift (see page 121).

🔺 *The bustling 2100 area interchange*

SNOW PARKS

Alpe d'Huez boasts two separate Snow Parks, both within easy reach of town and both reasonably well-maintained, with a fair range of modules between them.

🔺 *Heading for the main Snow Park*

The main park is an interloper at the heart of the Jeux beginners' zone. To reach it, take the Grandes Rousses (DMC) cable car or the Jeux button lifts from the Rond Point des Pistes; alternatively, the park is served specifically by the Babars I button lift from the base of the beginners' zone, but this is a hike away from the main base area. The park covers an extensive area and delivers a decent in-line run, the only downside being the long flat exit towards the lifts and the base area again.

The secondary park is located next to the Lac Blanc button lift, which provides uplift for park users. This smaller park has a more limited range of modules, but it features some huge launch pads and it exits close to the Rond Point des Pistes area, making it more convenient for the lifts.

The nearest bar/restaurant to the main park is La Plage des Neiges at the top of the Babars button lift; the second park is handy to the well-serviced Rond Point des Pistes base area.

COMBINED MODULES

- Boarder/SkierCross course
- Flat/flat-down rails
- Various big air kickers
- Tabletops
- Halfpipe
- Flat boxes
- Flat rails

MARMOTTES I GONDOLA LIFT

 9 mins

- 525 m (1723 ft) vertical rise
- 2243 m (2454 yd) long
- 2200 passengers/hour

The key lift out of the Bergers base area, accessing the upper Town sector slopes, linking with the Marmottes II gondola lift into the Mid sector and, via a further link with the Marmottes III cable car, providing a secondary route to the Glacier de Sarenne on Pic Blanc.

The lift station is located immediately behind the Bergers commercial centre and is a large structure raised high off the ground, with ramps leading up to the departure platform. There are plenty of gear racks around the base of the structure and in the surrounding area. A full-area piste map display and link-lifts information board is positioned along with current avalanche risk-level warnings at the approach area to the access ramps. Ski pass sales points are within the commercial centre, easily accessible on foot from the piste level.

The external gear holders on the cabins are poorly designed: when snowboards are slotted in, they block the ski holders behind – so if you are with a mixed discipline group, put skis in first!

The journey up gives sweeping views over virtually the entire Town sector, the whole town and towards the peaks of the Ecrins National Park beyond. On arrival, dismount and either go straight ahead on this same level to access the separate Marmottes II gondola lift to continue the journey (see page 126), or exit the arrival platform down the access ramp to the right.

This level is the 2300 area interchange (see page 112 for onward routes) and is right next to the huge Marmottes panoramic terrace bar/restaurant (see page 224).

2300 AREA INTERCHANGE

Also known as the Plat des Marmottes, this compact plateau at the interchange for the Marmottes I and II gondola lifts is the highest-altitude lift and piste crossover point in this sector. It can also be reached on piste from the upper Mid sector, via the Boulevard des Marmottes blue from the Couloir blue (see page 120) and the Déversoir red (see page 122).

At 2300 m (7544 ft), the area offers a respectable vertical drop and a correspondingly decent selection of good varied runs back to base, including the station's Super Giant competition course (the Vachettes piste – see over). This altitude also permits efficient on-piste links to the 2100 area interchange, opening up access to all core sectors. The Marmottes II gondola lift (see page 126) accesses the testing reds and blacks in the upper Mid sector and connects with the Marmottes III cable car to reach the glacial zone and epic Sarenne run on Pic Blanc.

The plateau is dominated by the large lift-station structure and the huge Marmottes bar/restaurant (see page 224). There are lots of deckchairs set out on the snow between the lifts and the restaurant but the terrace is the main feature: a huge platform cantilevered off the mountainside, effectively creating an artificial extension to the plateau. On a clear day, the panoramic views over the core ski sectors and town are superb, extending over Auris and as far as Les Deux Alpes in its high hanging valley to the distant left. A piste patrol information/first-aid cabin is situated on the ground level next to the access ramps for the lifts and there is a centrally positioned piste map and good directional signage.

The pistes starting from this point flow off both sides of the plateau, dropping over each side of the watershed to head either towards the Bergers base area (Vachettes blue and Olympique red) or in the direction of the 2100 area interchange (Dahut blue, Poutat and La Course reds). Pedestrians and novices can of course simply opt to ride the Marmottes I gondola lift down to town.

DAHUT

This short and efficient link makes the most accessible connection between the 2300 and 2100 area interchanges. From the Plat des Marmottes, pass under the lifts station structure to the side furthest away from the restaurant; the pisted access track is flat and wide. Once clear of the lifts there is a junction point for the Poutat red, which drops away to the left; keep straight on for the Dahut. The route then really gets going with a short mild red pitch, manageable by confident and competent novices, and crossing under the line of the Lievre Blanc chair lift before running out to join the Couloir blue (see page 120) for the onward cruise towards the 2100 area interchange.

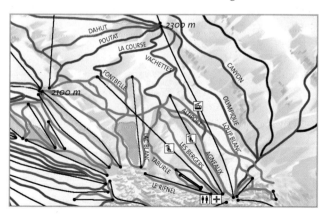

POUTAT

The Poutat begins alongside the Dahut blue, gliding under the lifts' structure away from the Plat des Marmottes to the point where it then parts company with the Dahut and drops off on to the steeper face of the hillside to the left. The route is really a wilder twin of the Dahut, with a more direct fall-line descent over bumpier and more sparsely covered ground. Ride out to the left or right for the deepest pockets and to up the ante by tackling the low rocky drop-offs. Veering to the right across the hill, the route eventually meets the lowermost section of the wide Couloir blue to finish as an easy cruise towards the 2100 area interchange. For intermediate and advanced visitors, this route offers one of the best links from this side of the station towards the 2100 area interchange, allowing maximum link options to all other sectors.

LA COURSE

A run that's very similar in profile to the Poutat red, on the same steep face of the hillside beneath the Plat des Marmottes, but it begins by passing under the line of the arriving Marmottes I gondola lift at the front of the lift structure, nearest to the restaurant's deckchair ranks. Once clear of the lift structure the route then drops down on to the face of the hillside, parallel to the lift-line, before veering to the right across the steep and testing slope, with a fairly aggressive angle of descent. After a few twists and turns through the rocky outcrops, this short route ends by dropping out to join the Fontbelle green piste a little way past the arrival point of the Fontbelle chair lift. Although La Course ends here, the onward descent leads towards the lower Snow Park, parallel to the Lac Blanc button lift.

VACHETTES

This is the resort's Giant Slalom competition course and is consequently a well-maintained fast cruise, flowing off the Plat des Marmottes as a wide, high-end blue down the left-hand side of the restaurant buildings. The start is shared with the Olympique red, which departs to the left at the first bend below; the Vachettes swings to the right, below the huge overhanging terrace of the restaurant, and runs under the line of the gondola lift before swooping down to the left to continue twisting along the broad gullied route of the competition course. After its fast and snaking run, the route emerges on to the top of the vast green motorways above the Bergers base area. A spur leads off to the left to the nearby good La Cabane de Poutat chalet restaurant (see page 225), otherwise, simply keep straight ahead to merge into the beginners zone above the Bergers base area.

OLYMPIQUE

This course is accessed off to the left of the Vachettes blue, at the specially provided gaps in the catch netting at the side of the competition course; drop in at the earliest opportunity for the steepest line. The route is a fair-to-good red, but there is also plenty of opportunity to ride up the steep sidewalls, and keeping high to the right also accesses some challenging freeride with high rocky drop-offs – stay focused and plan your line well. This direction emerges behind La Cabane de Poutat chalet restaurant (see page 225).

The main piste twists quickly through the gullied route, before veering off to the left as a mellow schuss to merge with the other home run pistes towards the Altiport and Bergers base area.

ALPE D'HUEZ MID SKI SECTOR

Above the 2100 and 2300 area interchanges, the lift network continues upwards on to the higher flanks of Pic Blanc to access a range of much more varied terrain and the core ski area's first really interesting cruises. All are still within sight of the resort and can be linked with any of the town sector slopes to provide home runs.

GRANDES ROUSSES (DMC) CABLE CAR – 2ème TRONÇON

 8¹/₄ mins

- 600 m (1969 ft) vertical rise
- 3000 passengers/hour

The second section of Alpe d'Huez's principal lift, accessed either by simply remaining in the cabin if travelling up from the base station, or by embarking at the 2100 area mid-station. The cabins declutch through this mid-station, taking two minutes to clear the building. The waiting time for embarkation can be considerable here if the cabins are full from the base station.

The journey up gives a bird's-eye view over the Nordic and snowmobile circuits on the frozen lake below left and up the Mid-sector slopes to the right, particularly the steep Chamois red piste directly below right.

On arrival at the upper-station, exit the cabins quickly as they turn sharply to return down. The arrival area is fairly spacious, with a tool point to the left beside frequently updated information boards. Exit to the right down the ramp to access the pistes and the Grotte de Glace ice cave, or to join the separate queue line back into the station for the Pic Blanc cable car.

◀ *Moody late afternoon light over Alpe d'Huez, viewed from the 2700 area*

2700 AREA INTERCHANGE

This interchange is centred around the shared Grandes Rousses (DMC) and Pic Blanc cable cars' station. There are WCs within the station building and a first-aid and information point at the piste patrol cabin on the pisted plateau in front. The Grotte de Glace ice cave (see page 239) is just behind the lifts' station and the Lac Blanc chair lift arrives just above this area; the pisted link track from its arrival point merges on to the plateau just next to the ice cave. Le Dôme and Le Belvédère red pistes, linking from the arrival point of the Alpette-Rousses cable car at the summit of the Dôme des Petites Rousses, also flow into this area.

Three pistes depart from this level: Les Rousses red (see page 180) towards Oz and Vaujany starts next to the Grotte de Glace; the Chamois red and Couloir blue pistes flow off the plateau in front of the lifts' station, into the main Alpe d'Huez sectors and towards a further couple of entrances for Les Rousses red.

⬤ The busy 2700 area lifts and pistes interchange

CHAMOIS

This good red shares its start with the Couloir blue, flowing off the front of the 2700 area plateau as a wide but often busy and choppy funnel, swinging down to run parallel to the left of the Grandes Rousses (DMC) cable car line. Keep to the right-hand side of the piste for the steepest ride. The Chamois peels off to the right, at a wide junction that is also a shared alternative entrance for Les Rousses red. This shared access route sweeps to the right across the mountainside: Les Rousses continues traversing to cross under the line of the cable car; the Chamois red drops sharp left, directly under the lift line, on to the steep fall line to earn its true red status. This often mogulled pitch is in full view of the cable car passengers, so descend as stylishly as you can.

Although this section is only around 100 m (109 yd) long, it is often a real challenge. Check your speed, though, and watch for crossing traffic ahead, because a second and final alternative entrance for Les Rousses red comes in from the left and cuts straight across your line of descent.

Carefully cross the line of Les Rousses, to continue straight off the lip of the track to resume the steep fall-line descent, still directly under the cable car line. This lower section is now the final pitch of the run, but keeps the challenge level high, often heavily mogulled and now narrowing down this cliff-top chute. The 2100 interchange area is visible directly below.

The Chamois rapidly mellows in gradient and requires a fast schuss to run along the side of the lake plateau to reach the lifts/onward piste links and Chantebise 2100 (see page 222) restaurant ahead. It is also possible to carefully veer right and traverse behind the restaurant to reach the Poutran red towards Oz-en-Oisans.

COULOIR

From its shared start with the Chamois red piste (see previous page), off the 2700 area plateau, the Couloir blue stays central down the mild red-profile fall-line; stay widest left for the gentlest gradient. The Chamois and Les Rousses reds leave to the right at the first wide junction; veer left to remain on the Couloir. The run funnels into a wide gully, giving plenty of opportunity to play up the sides. Another exit to the right just below is the final alternative route for Les Rousses red, leaving towards Oz and Vaujany. The Couloir is an enjoyable tough blue, following the line of the long, wide gully after which it is named, with frequent small moguls and kickers built up around the centrally positioned snowmaking cannons – inviting launch-offs.

The Lièvre Blanc red drops in from the rockier and steeper slopes above left, just before a wide junction: swing left to take the long, flat Boulevard des Marmottes blue link track towards the 2300 interchange area for the Marmottes restaurant and Marmottes I/II gondolas mid-station, or remain central right to continue on the Couloir blue.

The Couloir maintains its pace as a wide and fast cruise, normally with plenty of wind-blown kickers and snowdrift lips to play off on the right-hand side. As you approach the line of the overhead Lièvre Blanc chair lift, the Dahut and Poutat pistes join from above left and you have a choice at the next well-signed junction ahead: either turn left on to the pisted link track to head towards the Bergers area of Alpe d'Huez via the Centrale and Retour Bergers green pistes; or, veer right to remain on the final pitch of the Couloir, which schusses out towards the busy 2100 interchange area. Keep right to reach the cable car station and restaurant; keep left to link with the Lièvre Blanc chair lift.

LIÈVRE BLANC CHAIR LIFT

11 mins   • 448 m (1470 ft) vertical rise

Departing from the 2100 area, around 100 m (109 yds) in front of the Chantebise 2100 restaurant and Grandes Rousses (DMC) cable car mid-station. The lift is easily reached from the end of the Couloir blue piste and is a gentle glide from the restaurant. It is a less busy alternative to the DMC for this upper Mid sector, although it does not make a connection towards Vaujany.

The journey up travels over the main snow-making plant reservoirs. The lines of bubbles that break the surface are produced by an underwater pipe system designed to agitate the water to prevent the ponds from freezing over.

On arrival, dismount straight ahead. There is a first-aid and information cabin immediately left and a piste map and electronic information display to the right. The Clocher de Macle black run is the piste descending towards you from above. This arrival point is at a watershed on these upper rocky slopes, giving two possible onward routes: to the left, around the back of the lift anchor pylon, is the start of the Lièvre Blanc red; to the right is the start of the Déversoir and Canyon reds, leading towards La Balme black.

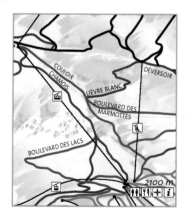

LIÈVRE BLANC

Starts from the Lièvre Blanc chair lift arrival point, as a wide fair red. After just 50 m (55 yds), there is a lovely steep couloir off to the right which rejoins the piste further below and is well worth investigation if you want to up the ante on this fairly short descent. The piste itself has some enjoyable wind-blown kickers and boulder drop-offs, particularly on the right-hand side (❶ caution – do not stray too far to the right: the ropes mark the edge of a sheer drop). The route then turns right to traverse across the mountainside and follows an uneventful link track to join the Couloir blue. The Lièvre Blanc ends here and all onward options are as per the Couloir piste.

DÉVERSOIR

Begins sharp to the right on arrival from the Lièvre Blanc chair lift, or as a continuation of the Clocher de Macle black. The top section is really just a blue equivalent, traversing under the line of the gondola before picking up a more useful slope angle. A great alternative is to turn sharply to the right into the steep fall-line chute that drops down to rejoin the main route below and that can be linked with the Canyon red to deliver the most challenging descent possible from this route. The Déversoir continues sweeping out to the left, curving down to an easy junction for La Balme black, before swinging to the right on to its steepest and most testing, albeit short, section – look out for traffic exiting and crossing from the steep chute above right. A sharp bend to the left then takes the Déversoir on to a bland, contour-hugging track towards the 2300 interchange area, but the Canyon red drops off severely and invitingly to the left.

CANYON

This begins as the Déversoir red, from the top of the Lièvre Blanc chair lift or as a continuation of the Clocher de Macle black run from the top of the Marmottes II gondola. The highest and most challenging start is to leave the Déversoir piste to the right at its uppermost traverse, straight after it passes under the Marmottes II gondola travelling overhead. This begins a steep, direct fall-line chute and delivers the longest and most testing descent.

The chute drops out below to cross the line of the Déversoir at a narrow, tight bend, where the Canyon officially begins by dropping straight down into a steep, narrow gully. This is one of the toughest routes in this sector, equivalent to a decent black.

After some 300 m (328 yds), the slope angle lessens and the Canyon widens out to become a fast, long and interesting red, running around the lower flanks of Pic Blanc towards the Altiport at the Bergers area of Alpe d'Huez, with sweeping views to the right over the resort and lower sectors as you cruise round. The Canyon ends when it merges with the Campanules and Olympique reds, running past the attractive Altiport chalets' suburb towards the Bergers commercial centre and the Marmottes I gondola base station.

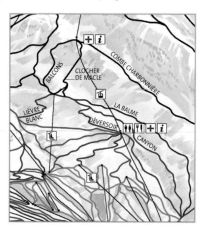

LA BALME

To access this quiet but enjoyable fast cruise, you need to take the mild Déversoir red, either from the top of the Lièvre Blanc chair lift or simply as a continuation of the Clocher de Macle black if you are coming from the top of the Marmottes II gondola. The entrance to La Balme black is off to the left, just before the Déversoir swings to the right after its fairly gentle upper section. La Balme's start area is wide and well signed, but is very flat and really is a green equivalent for the 70–80 m (77–87 yds) it takes to reach the true start of the descent. The piste then drops away with a more respectable fair red profile on the steeper flanks of the mountainside, affording great views ahead towards the Auris sector and to the right over the Plat des Marmottes area towards Alpe d'Huez and over almost all of the town sector slopes. The route takes a direct line off the shoulder of the hill, narrowing through the rocky outcrop ahead, often with wind-blown kickers to pop off at the sides, emerging on to a mild-to-fair black pitch for the next 150 m (164 yds) and presenting more varied riding options on a wider and more open slope.

The lower section becomes increasingly mellow in gradient, inviting a fast schuss towards the official finish of La Balme ahead, where it merges with the Campanules red piste coming in from above left. The onward descent towards the Bergers area of Alpe d'Huez is as per the Campanules piste; however, there is an interesting little river gully to the right just before the pistes merge which is worth a look in if conditions are right, although it does require a bit of work to get out of it again at the bottom.

___

▶ *Peaceful cruising on La Balme black piste*

MARMOTTES II GONDOLA LIFT

5¼ mins ▲▼   • 500 m (1641 ft) vertical rise

This second section of this principal gondola lift is accessible either on arrival from the Marmottes I gondola, by remaining on the shared lift platform and walking straight ahead through the onward turnstiles, or from the Plat des Marmottes 2300 area, from the end of the Déversoir red or Boulevard des Marmottes blue pistes, beside the Marmottes restaurant.

The journey up gives good views over the entire resort and town sector slopes. On arrival, dismount from the arrival platform directly on to the snow. There is a piste-patrol first-aid cabin on the left. From this pisted arrival area at 2800 m (9187 ft), you can either walk around the lift structure to reach the separate access ramp ahead for the Marmottes III cable car towards the Glacier de Sarenne, or put your gear on to begin the descent from here for the highest start in this sector. The pistes beginning here are all black: the Balcons run is to the far left, past the lift structure; the Combe Charbonnière and Clocher de Macle runs flow off to the right.

BALCONS

Accessed by walking around the far side of the lift structure at the 2800 area interchange, and dropping off on to the severely steep and rocky slopes directly beneath the lift cables. This top section of the descent is inviting, but it is really not worth the effort because it is no more than 200 m (219 yds) long and runs out to stop abruptly on the flat shoreline of the small Lac Blanc tarn below, requiring a long hike to exit the area.

CLOCHER DE MACLE ●

This is the short, steep route visible below right as you arrive on the Marmottes II gondola. From the lift's arrival area, the piste swings down to the right with a very good red-equivalent profile down the fall-line; a good alternative is to ride out higher to the right and then drop off on to the even steeper and deeper slopes above the piste. The gradient mellows as it runs under the lift line, to a wide junction below near the arriving Lièvre Blanc chair lift. Keep right to ride over the high ground by the lift to reach the Lièvre Blanc red piste beyond, or keep descending and veer left to link with the Déversoir red and to access the Canyon red and La Balme black.

COMBE CHARBONNIÈRE ●

A promising-looking long black, high on the flanks of Pic Blanc. Unfortunately, the access track is often bare and therefore seldom open; if you are lucky enough to visit when it is accessible, then it is definitely worth a go. The route begins alongside the Clocher de Macle piste, but then immediately traverses out high and flat to the left. Once past this high ground, the run truly begins, cruising along the base of the cliffs with a mild-to-fair red profile, high above the rest of the ski area and with great views over it.

The lower section is the steepest and widest part of the run, presenting lots of possible lines of descent on the open and ungroomed slopes above the Chalvet chair lift arrival area. Head towards this lift to join either the Campanules or La Mine red pistes: the Campanules heads to the right towards the Bergers area of Alpe d'Huez, while La Mine continues the descent ahead left down into the Gorges de Sarenne.

PIC BLANC SKI SECTOR

This is Alpe d'Huez's crowning glory, home to its highest altitude ski area and its most thrilling descents, including the world's longest Alpine piste – the Sarenne black.

The summit can be reached easily by skiers and non-skiers; the 360-degree panorama from the peak is breathtaking and takes in a reputed one-fifth of France, plus quite a chunk of north-west Italy and south-west Switzerland. Two major lifts access this sector: the Marmottes III cable car and the Pic Blanc cable car.

MARMOTTES III CABLE CAR

 3¼ mins ▲▼

- 300 m (984 ft) vertical rise
- 1075 passengers/hour

This fast twin-cabin cable car gives access to the 3060 m (10,037 ft) level at the mid point of the Glacier de Sarenne, avoiding the busier summit area. The lift departs from the Clocher de Macle 2800 interchange, reached via the Marmottes II gondola lift. The journey up gives bird's eye views of virtually all of Alpe d'Huez's core ski sectors and of the cliffs of the Pic Blanc massif ahead.

On arrival, exit the station building ahead right; there are WCs and a tool point just before the exit. The Herpie chair lift also arrives at this altitude; the Cristaux black, Cristallière blue, Hermine red and Herpie blue pistes all begin here too, flowing down to the right parallel to the chair lift. Alternatively, follow the gentle link track ahead past the chair lift arrival point around the contour-line to the Glacier chair lift to continue on to the summit of Pic Blanc.

◉ *Preparing to start the glacier runs, Pic Blanc summit*

PIC BLANC CABLE CAR

5 mins ▲▼

- 696 m (2284 ft) vertical rise
- 2126 m (2326 yd) long
- 1000 passengers/hour

The principal uplift to the summit of Pic Blanc, accessible by all visitors to reach one of the most spectacular viewpoints in the Alps, as well as all upper slopes on the Glacier de Sarenne. The cable car departs from the 2700 area interchange, from a station building shared with the upper section of the Grandes Rousses (DMC) cable car. This area is also reachable on-piste via the Pic Blanc Tunnel black runs and by Le Dôme red piste linking from the Alpette-Rousses cable car. The departure platform is mobile, moving slowly from side-to-side to fill the void left by the departing cabin and to accommodate the arriving cabin on the opposite side. There's no need to rush to be first on; last person on is first off!

The vertiginous journey up affords good views over the Alpe d'Huez mid sector and allows you to study the lines of the Pic Blanc Tunnel black runs emerging from the cliff-face tunnel below right.

On arrival, there is a tool point to the right just before the station exit. Immediately outside the building you step on to a spacious viewing platform; access to the pistes is via a narrow track starting at the rear of the platform.

🔺 *Pic Blanc cable car*

SUMMIT ORIENTATION

This high-altitude realm of rock and ice is subject to its own micro-climate and frequently exposed to high winds and severe weather, forcing the lifts to close even when conditions are fine in the lower sectors; on most days, however, it offers Alpe d'Huez's most exciting and snow-sure pistes, against a stunning backdrop.

The viewing platform at the cable car arrival area affords sweeping views over Alpe d'Huez and the peaks of the Ecrins National Park, but the best viewpoint is on the summit itself, accessed via a short flight of icy steps behind the lift station. From here, on a clear day, Mont Blanc is visible on the horizon ahead left and the instantly recognizable triple-peaked Aiguilles d'Arves is ahead right. Ninety degrees to the right of the Aiguilles d'Arves is the resort of Les Deux Alpes, nestling in a high valley beyond Auris.

All pistes begin via a narrow access track from the rear of the main viewing platform, heading off along the side of the summit for 20–30 m (22–33 yd), before turning sharply down to the right and widening out on to the uppermost section of the glacier. The serious off-piste routes via the Glacier du Grand Sablat, Pic Bayle and Col des Quirlies are all also reached from here. Alternatively, a long flight of metal stairs from the side of the viewing platform links with the arrival point of the Glacier chair lift, passing a piste patrol and first-aid cabin on a mezzanine level. You can use these steps to avoid the bottleneck at the summit and to join all upper glacier pistes from this slightly lower, marginally easier start area.

🛈 Caution: Pic Blanc summit is at 3,330 m (10,922 ft) altitude and can be very exposed, experiencing rapid changes in weather – dress for extreme conditions even if it's a fair-weather day or if you are only visiting the viewpoint.

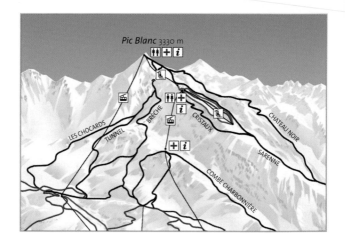

GLACIER DE SARENNE

Once past the Pic Blanc summit area access track you reach the same level as the arriving Glacier chair lift, which rises on the right from the gentler mid-point of the glacier bowl. This shared start area then fans out on to the glacial slopes, presenting three principal choices for onward descent: turn right at either the first or second piste junction to access the Pic Blanc Tunnel, towards the Tunnel, Les Chocards and Brèche black runs (see page 134) back into the core Alpe d'Huez sectors; keep straight ahead for the prime Sarenne piste; or, take the gentler pisted track leading wide out to the left to access the quieter and wider Château Noir piste at the far side of the high ground ahead.

All the upper glacier runs are graded black. They are really fair red equivalent in gradient profile, but the wind-whipped and hard-packed icy surface does make them more testing. All are variations of the Sarenne piste and all can be linked to the epic 17 km (10¹/₂ mile) summit-to-valley descent (see page 139).

The steepest line on the uppermost slopes is achieved by keeping furthest to the right, with the first branch off towards the Pic Blanc Tunnel providing the truest black-profile descent. As well as linking with the tunnel entrance, this direction also leads to the wide fast straight called the Glacier piste, which runs down the right-hand side of the glacier as another quieter variation of the Sarenne piste.

All route variations finally funnel together at the base of the glacier to flow gently out of the summit area, parallel to the line of the lower Herpie chair lift, to continue as the Sarenne run. The Herpie chair lift serves a cluster of four further glacial pistes (the Cristallière and Herpie blues, Hermine red and Cristaux black – see pages 137–38) and can be linked with the Marmottes III cable car to return to the core Alpe d'Huez sectors, or with the Glacier chair lift to return to the summit of Pic Blanc. Once past the get-on level of the Herpie chair lift, you are committed to the full Sarenne run.

CAUTION

You are now on a glacier, where dangerous crevasses are numerous even if you can't see them. The piste patrol have clearly marked out the pistes and you are strongly advised to stay on them.

If you take off your skis or board, you become simply an un-roped pedestrian in a serious mountaineering environment, so keep your gear on at all times when moving around on the glacier.

TUNNEL / BRÈCHE / LES CHOCARDS

Along with the Sarenne piste, the Tunnel runs are Alpe d'Huez's most emblematic and notorious routes, providing the station's most severe on-piste challenges. From the shared Pic Blanc summit area, keep to the right-hand side of the piste and take the first junction to the right after just 100 m (109 yd). The next short section down towards the Pic Blanc Tunnel is the most testing slope on the glacier, with frequent moguls and wind-blown ridges; it crosses under the chair lift line and drops down to join a narrow link track coming from an easier second junction below.

The tunnel entrance is just a hut plonked in the middle of the mountainside; slow up on your approach and carefully skate in through the cramped doorway. The narrow, dimly lit tunnel is 200 m (219 yd) long, penetrating straight through the mountain to emerge on the far side of the arête. The floor is pisted, with a slight downhill gradient and a simple rope handrail, but it's still a bit of a slog. Emerging at the other end, it takes a moment for your eyes to adjust to the daylight again, then the severity of this exposed route quickly becomes clear: exiting to the right on to a narrow traverse track, which is effectively a ledge on the cliff face, the onward route almost immediately drops away on to a very steep and often heavily mogulled icy slope. A narrow, and still tricky, escape track has been cut into the slope out to the right to take the sting out of this truly tough pitch.

After the adrenaline buzz of the difficult tunnel exit pitch, the piste widens out on to a much more manageable slope, still with a good black profile and offering a choice of routes: keep highest left to ride out on the contour-line over the ridge ahead for the Brèche route; or, stay central and right to continue on the Tunnel piste and towards Les Chocards variation route.

The Brèche reaches a fairly enjoyable short steep pitch above Lac Blanc, but it's a bit of a slog to get to and also requires a hike to exit. Wide to the right, Les Chocards wanders off over undulating open ground on that side of the hill, but it's very tame and often indistinctly route-marked. The central Tunnel piste delivers the best descent, swinging to the right across the mountainside and giving a good workout before turning down onto the fall-line for a fast schuss: check your speed as you approach the blind crest ahead.

● *The crux of the notorious Tunnel run*

The piste then fans out on to a wider, good red-equivalent slope, steadily mellowing in gradient and requiring a schuss over a long flat section below.

A junction off to the right links over to the Dolomits and Le Dôme reds; joining the flat Le Dôme traverse track saves having to take the Lac Blanc chair lift to reach the 2700 area interchange, but there's no real advantage in doing so and the Tunnel piste still has more to give. Once past this flat section, the Tunnel run veers to the left and picks up a good red profile again as it drops for its final fast blast down to link well with the Lac Blanc chair lift below. The twin profile piste running down parallel to the right here is the Dolomits red.

HERPIE CHAIR LIFT

4 · ☒ · 7¼ mins

- 328 m (1076 ft) vertical rise
- 993 m (1086 yd) long
- 2000 passengers/hour

Departing from 2736 m (8974 ft) on the lower reaches of the Glacier de Sarenne and providing the final opportunity to return to the major lifts on Pic Blanc; below this point the sole exit route off the mountain is the Sarenne black piste all the way down to link with the Chalvet, Lombards or Alpauris chair lifts in the deep Gorges de Sarenne below Alpe d'Huez and Auris.

The journey up gives good views over the four lower glacier pistes, which descend parallel to the lift line, as well as up ahead right over the main glacier zone towards the summit of Pic Blanc.

On arrival, the Marmottes III cable car upper station is immediately to the left; to the right is the start of all lower glacier pistes; plus a long, very gentle blue link track following the contour-line across the mountain to link with the Glacier chair lift towards the upper glacier slopes and the summit. If the Glacier chair lift is closed, you will have to walk back around to the Marmottes III cable car, or descend via the Sarenne piste.

The pistes at the top of the Herpie lift are, from right to left from their shared start area looking down the lift line: the Cristaux black, the Cristallière blue, the Hermine red, and the Herpie blue.

Pic Blanc 3330 m

HERPIE
HERMINE
SARENNE
CRISTALLIERE
CRISTAUX

GLACIER CHAIR LIFT

| 7¾ mins | • 368 m (1207 ft) vertical rise
• 960 m (1050 yd) long
• 1600 passengers/hour |

The sole lift serving the upper glacier slopes and providing uplift towards the summit of Pic Blanc. The lift is located bang in the middle of the wide central glacier zone, reachable from all upper piste variations. The journey up affords sweeping views over the glacier, up towards the summit and the Pic Blanc Tunnel disappearing into the mountainside ahead left.

On arrival, turn sharp right to immediately join the shared access piste for all routes on the upper glacier; alternatively, turn left and walk up the long metal staircase to reach the Pic Blanc summit viewing platform and cable car station; there is a piste patrol/first-aid cabin on a mezzanine level on these stairs.

HERPIE

This short piste follows the start of the link track towards the Glacier chair lift, from the Marmottes III cable car and the Herpie chair lift arrival points, before flowing off down to the right to link with the gentlest part of the Sarenne piste. This route is really just a link to the Sarenne, but officially it continues with the Sarenne run down to the get-on level of the Herpie chair lift, so confident and competent novices could ski this route and then boast that they've skied both on a glacier and on part of a black run! Only good intermediates and above should proceed below the base of the Herpie lift though, as the only onward descent from that point is via the full-on Sarenne black run, which goes on to develop into a much more ambitious challenge.

HERMINE

This starts at the top of the Herpie chair lift and runs down parallel to the left of the lift line. It is a decent, direct, fast red, flowing down the side of the glacier to access the base of the Herpie chair lift, with the option of continuing past the lift get-on level to link with the most enjoyable and challenging lower sections of the principal Sarenne black descent.

CRISTALLIÈRE

Although graded as a blue, this enjoyable run is basically a twin of the parallel Hermine red and shares the slope with the Cristaux black! It starts at the top of the Herpie chair lift and runs down the right-hand side of the lift line, undulating over some decent steeper sections on the side of the glacier; the hard-packed surface often boosts the difficulty level to a fairly consistent mild red standard all the way down to the base of the chair lift. Below the chair lift level you are committed to the full Sarenne descent.

CRISTAUX

Beginning with and running alongside the Cristallière blue run, but taking a steeper line out on the furthest reaches of the glacier to the far right. Much of the run is equivalent to a fair-to-good red despite its grade as a black. It merges with the Cristallière blue again below, providing a good link with the Herpie chair lift, but also continues past this level as a fast and frequently mogulled, good red-equivalent blast; joining the main Sarenne run further below for the onward long descent into the deep Gorges de Sarenne.

SARENNE ●

Alpe d'Huez's signature run, said to be the world's longest Alpine piste, extending for an incredible 17 km (10½ miles) with 1820 m (5970 ft) of vertical drop. You may imagine that a piste of this extent meanders down the mountain with a very shallow slope angle, but the Sarenne maintains a fairly consistent fall-line descent and a respectable gradient for all but its final section. Overall it is equivalent to a fair-to-good red, but its sheer length and isolation qualify it as a fair black. The route is well-maintained and easy to follow, and should feature in the plans of all visitors who are at least of competent intermediate ability.

The run officially starts on the shared access track from the rear of the viewing platform at Pic Blanc summit. All of the uppermost glacier pistes from here are regarded as variations of the Sarenne, but the main route is the central icy motorway, giving the steepest and fastest run into the open glacial bowl, parallel to the line of the Glacier chair lift. Past this lift's get-on point (easy link), all variations come together to continue as a flat straight track flowing off the glacier – schuss to keep momentum. A branch to the right links to the Herpie chair lift; this also allows you to join the Cristaux black to continue past the lift get-on point as a generally much quieter and worthwhile twin of the prime route, eventually merging again with the parallel Sarenne piste lower down. ❶ Once past the Herpie lift you are committed to the full Sarenne descent!

The Château Noir variation peels off here too, but it's a disappointing and seldom accessible variant, ranging out wide on the higher ground to the left; the Sarenne continues straight down with a much more enjoyable pace. A piste patrol/first-aid cabin is located at the point where the Château Noir eventually rejoins the main route below, on a rocky crest. The scenery here is wild and beautiful, with views directly ahead over the Auris sector towards the resort of Les Deux Alpes. Take care funnelling through this area and expect slow-moving traffic as people stop and restart from this popular viewpoint. Immediately below this level, the now lone Sarenne piste drops more steeply through twists and turns and narrower sections, all the way down the deep valley, with only a couple of mellower pitches to catch your breath.

The route finally widens out into an open bowl below the Col de Cluy, presenting a few options to finish off with a flourish – if you have the legs left for it! You can blast down the central marked piste; or, ride out wide left on the contour-line to reach the deeper snow in the middle of the bowl; or, ride high to the right for the steepest finish, eventually dropping down to rejoin the Sarenne just before it flattens out across the bridge ahead right. This little bridge is just beyond piste-marker number six and, although there are another couple of kilometres to go, the descent really peters out here. A long, flat, onward link track follows the route of the Sarennes River along the attractive, wooded valley floor, joined by the Auris sector's Col de Cluy and Le Gua pistes; as long as the snow conditions are not too slushy, it's a manageable skate to the lifts. The nearest link is the Chalvet chair lift (towards Alpe d'Huez), conveniently sited beside the excellent Combe Haute mountain restaurant for a reviving meal or drink after this epic run. The track also continues to the Auris sector's Lombards chair lift and runs all the way to the mid-station of the Alpauris chair lift (towards Alpe d'Huez only), but this is a real slog and gives no advantage.

▶ Rest stop on the epic Sarenne run

CHALVET CHAIR LIFT

12 mins

- 626 m (2054 ft) vertical rise
- 1650 m (1805 yd) long
- 1100 passengers/hour

Sited beside the Combe Haute restaurant, this basic chair lift is the first link out of the Gorges de Sarenne when you're travelling from the Sarenne piste or from the Auris sector's Col de Cluy and Le Gua pistes. It provides the best link towards Alpe d'Huez from this area.

Rising steeply up imposing sheer cliffs, the lift journeys over tiers of frozen mini-waterfalls and ice-flows and affords great views over this spectacular setting. Look over your left shoulder for a sweeping view up the lines of the Lombards and Fontfroide chair lifts and the parallel steep red pistes in neighbouring Auris sector.

On arrival, turn left for all onward routes: U-turn to the left to start La Mine red piste back down into the Gorges de Sarenne to the base of this lift; or, follow the contour-line track straight across the mountainside to reach Alpe d'Huez's Altiport and Bergers base area, visible ahead, via the Campanules red piste.

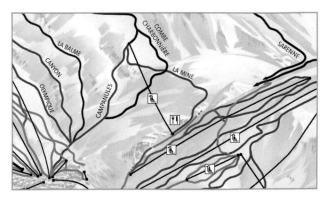

LA MINE ●

From the top of the Chalvet chair lift, this is the sole piste descending on this flank of the Gorges de Sarenne. The entire open snowfield under the uppermost section of the lift-line can be ridden, but the pisted route swings wide to the left and off the shoulder of the hill on to quiet, lightly wooded slopes down into the deep valley below; safely away from the precipitous cliffs which lurk below the lower section of the lift-line. The final section traverses to the right and follows the route of the Sarennes River to the Combe Haute restaurant and the Chalvet chair lift. It is also possible to continue along the valley-floor track to link with the Lombards chair lift into the Auris sector.

CAMPANULES ●

Linking from the top of the Chalvet chair lift, and from the end of the Combe Charbonnière black run, towards Alpe d'Huez. The initial part of the route is simply a gentle road-like traverse, but gives sweeping views over the surrounding area: Alpe d'Huez is directly ahead, the Auris sector's main ski area is just opposite on the other side of the gorge, and the resort of Les Deux Alpes is distant left.

The piste eventually drops off on to the open hillside, heading straight in the direction of Alpe d'Huez as a much more enjoyable mild red. The slope angle gradually diminishes, inviting a long schuss over the gently undulating terrain ahead, joined from above right by pistes from the main Alpe d'Huez sectors. The Altiport chalets suburb is easily reachable via a wide pisted junction to the left; the Campanules continues straight on, merging with the green-graded superpistes running parallel to the line of the Marmottes I gondola lift to finish at the Bergers base area.

SIGNAL / VILLARD SKI SECTOR

In many respects the Signal hill is regarded as another segment of Alpe d'Huez's main Town sector: it rises immediately above the Vieil Alpe and Cognet quarters of town and its lower slopes are an integral part of the busy Rond Point des Pistes base hub. Its main lifts cluster around the upper station of the Télécentre bucket lift and the principal slopes run straight back down to town; this side of the hill serves as the resort's competition stadium and is dramatically floodlit for night skiing (see page 240). On the western flanks are a couple of really worthwhile reds, plus several enjoyable cruises down to the lift-linked village of Villard-Reculas.

SIGNAL CHAIR LIFT

5³/₄ mins

- 253 m (830 ft) vertical rise
- 815 m (892 yd) long
- 2050 passengers/hour

The principal lift serving the Signal hill from Alpe d'Huez, rising from the area immediately next to the Télécentre bucket lift station at the Rond Point des Pistes. The get-on area is shared with the parallel triple Signal button lifts: queue to the left for the button lifts, which are the fastest option for good skiers. All these lifts serve the competition stadium; the Signal piste to the left is floodlit and open to the public for night skiing (see page 240).

On arrival, turn right for the Signal Bis and KL reds and the Anémones blue. Go straight ahead veering right for the Hirondelles blue; or, turn left for all other routes, including those towards Villard-Reculas.

❶ These lifts will be replaced by a fast declutchable chair lift in 2007.

◀ *Taking in the view from the Petite Sure piste on the Signal*

145

SIGNAL SUMMIT ORIENTATION

At a relatively modest 2115 m (6937 ft), the summit of the Signal, or to give it its full title le Signal de la Grande Sure, is far from the highest vantage point in the area. However, it does offer an exceptional 360 degree panorama over Alpe d'Huez and the surrounding Grandes Rousses domain.

The summit plateau has three distinct levels, focused around the arrival points of the various lifts which serve this sector; a huge, centrally positioned piste map and information board aid orientation and route-finding, plus there is a piste patrol/first-aid hut. Looking down the lines of the parallel-running Signal triple button lifts and chair lift, your view is directly over Alpe d'Huez: the Rond Point des Pistes base hub is directly below you and the equally important Bergers base area is at the far side of town, ahead and left. In the distance ahead you can see the linked Auris sector ski area and, or a clear day, beyond that all the way over to the Glaciers du Monts-de-Lans above Les Deux Alpes. Up to your left is the huge core ski area, flowing down towards Alpe d'Huez from the flanks of Pic Blanc, the summit of which marks the highest lift-accessible point in the domain.

Turning to your right, Le Signal mountain restaurant is just off the Signal summit, close to the arrival points for the Grande Sure chair lift and Petit Prince twin button lifts. Huez village is below right and le Bourg-d'Oisans, the provincial capital, is down on the valley floor. The chair lift arriving over furthest right is the TSD Le Villarais linking from the village of Villard-Reculas, also linked by piste from here.

Behind you is the Eau-d'Olle valley, housing the lift- and piste-linked villages of Oz-en-Oisans and Vaujany, the latter nestling at the upper end of the valley beneath the Pic Blanc massif.

ANÉMONES / HIRONDELLES

Beginning closest to the Signal lifts' arrival area, these fair cruising routes range over the Signal's eastern side, nearest the core ski area. The Anémones starts right next to the Signal chair lift, traversing the front of the hill before picking up a mild red-equivalent gradient as it swoops off the summit. This short upper section is almost straight, dropping down to meet and join the Hirondelles piste below; check your speed and turn right to merge at the junction.

The Hirondelles has a slightly more circuitous and slightly less steep profile, wrapping round the rear of the summit before swinging right to where it is joined by the Anémones. Both routes then continue as one wide piste towards the Rond Point des Pistes. The mid section is a good blue, but the final long straight to town is very gentle and often requires a skate in softer conditions.

Limitations in representing topography on a two-dimensional plane mean that this side of the Signal seems compressed on the piste map; in fact the beginners' zone is separated from the Signal by a wide open hillside, covered by the parallel fast twin Stade pistes (served by the Sarrasins button lift) and the Boucle de Poutran Nordic circuit. The Stade pistes and Sarrasins button lift are easily accessed by dropping off the left-hand side of the Anémones/ Hirondelles mid section.

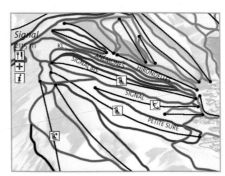

KL / SIGNAL BIS

Enjoyable parallel reds descending to the left of the Signal chair lift, on wide and open slopes frequently covered with moguls. The compressed projection of the piste map belies the extent of the slopes on this side of the hill, with lots of possible lines offering good freeriding on powder days. Both pistes are effectively twins and cover the same ground down this hillside. Both flow down to join the final gentle home stretch of the Anémones/Hirondelles blue piste towards the Rond Point des Pistes; schuss it to keep up momentum.

◔ *Signal night-skiing piste above Alpe d'Huez*

SIGNAL

Alpe d'Huez's principal slalom competition course and home to its floodlit night-skiing slopes (see also page 240), running straight down the face of the hill directly above town. Although marked as a single blue line on the local piste map, the piste is actually split into two: nearest the Signal button lifts is the main stadium piste; to the far right is the twin profile floodlit piste. Both maintain a good fall-line descent, equivalent to a mild-to-fair red, finishing at the base of the Signal and Stade lifts; check your speed before running out into the busy lifts base area at the Rond Point des Pistes.

STADE BUTTON LIFT

- 210 m (689 ft) vertical rise
- 705 m (771 yd) long
- 900 passengers/hour

Shortest lift on the face of the Signal, specifically serving the floodlit side of the Signal stadium. The base of the lift can be reached via the flat green-graded link track traversing above the uppermost part of town, alongside the line of the Télécentre bucket lift. You can also use the short Schuss button lift, rising from the roadside at the route du Signal, to gain height and allow you to traverse across to reach this lift.

On arrival at the top of the Stade, exit left to start the Petite Sure red; dismount to the right to join the Signal piste.

PETITE SURE

A really enjoyable, good red; often heavily mogulled and with a fast fall-line descent. The uppermost half is the steepest, providing a good workout on the bumpy terrain. The area out to the right has been planted to help stabilize the slopes and prevent avalanches so close to town; the regular rows of trees are an inviting diversion, but please respect this important young plantation. Once below the planted zone, you have two choices: either continue straight down towards town in the direction of the Tunnel des Grandes Rousses, or swing to the right to traverse across the lower slopes and skirt the town to reach the base of the Grande Sure chair lift and/or to join the route of the Village blue link track leading down to Huez village. The final approach to the Grande Sure lift can be very tricky – stick to the track cut out by the piste-groomer and check your speed.

GRANDE SURE CHAIR LIFT

9½ mins

- 352 m (1155 ft) vertical rise
- 930 m (1017 yd) long
- 500 passengers/hour

An older, slow lift up from the lower margins of the Vieil Alpe quarter, handy for good skiers staying at this side of the resort and wanting to get moving quickly in the mornings. It can be reached via the Petite Sure red piste and by dropping down off the Village blue track, or by using a piste-groomer link track opposite the Post Office on the route de la Poste. Take care on the final approach to the lift, the access track is steep and very narrow; get into position quickly when mounting the lift, as there is scant room to manoeuvre and the chairs turn rapidly around the base pylon mechanism, frequently bashing waiting passengers in the back of the legs!

The ride gives views up the Signal and over Alpe d'Huez, and allows you to see freeride lines through the young trees planted on the slope below to help prevent avalanches.

On arrival, Le Signal mountain restaurant is ahead right. Ahead left is a piste patrol/first-aid hut. Go right for all routes on the face of the Signal and to head for the Rond Point des Pistes; or, left for routes down to Villard-Reculas.

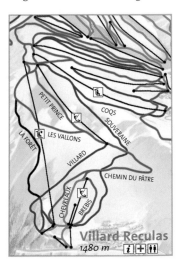

COQS / SOUVERAINE

Beginning as a spliced motorway-wide red from the top of the Signal, closest to the top of the Petit Prince button lift. The Souveraine leads the way, veering to the right in the direction of Villard-Reculas; the Coqs peels away to the left as you approach the ridge marking the watershed between Villard and Alpe d'Huez.

The Coqs heads towards the planted area to the left, eventually running almost parallel to the line of the Grande Sure chair lift. The piste is not particularly well maintained and is prone to closure; the upper and mid-sections are fair red, often ungroomed; finishing by running out to join the Village blue trail (you need to descend all the way down to Huez village in order to reach the nearest lift). The local piste map would appear to show the Coqs extending to the base of the Grande Sure chair lift, but this is not the case.

The Souveraine is a more reliable piste, taking a much better-maintained route parallel to the line of the Petit Prince twin button lifts, after the point where the Coqs departs to the left. The wide, straight upper section is an enjoyable cruise, down to the get-on level for the Petit Prince lifts; the route also continues past this level, swinging to the right below the lifts to cross the Chemin du Pâtre blue. The ground drops away very steeply ahead: either join the Chemin du Pâtre for a gentler hairpin cut into the hillside out to your left, or drop down through the narrow rocky gully ahead right for the most challenging descent – this brings you down to meet the Chemin du Pâtre again as it traverses across the slopes in the opposite direction. The Souveraine finishes as a broad, straight, mild red, widest out to the left, towards Villard-Reculas base directly below.

PETIT PRINCE / LES VALLONS / CHEMIN DU PÂTRE

Starting from the area between the arrival points of the Petit Prince button lifts and the TSD Le Villarais chair lift, and flowing off the Signal summit in the direction of Villard-Reculas.

Les Vallons takes the widest route out to the right, running under the line of the chair lift; the Petit Prince hugs the double line of its namesake button lifts. Both options are good blues, with a decent slope angle and plenty of scope to ride over the wide, open, inter-piste snowfields.

Where the terrain begins to steepen and become more gnarled, La Forêt black takes over for the direct descent; Les Vallons blue swings to the left, crossing under the chair lift line and traversing across to merge with the Petit Prince piste; continuing as one, parallel to the lower section of the Petit Prince button lifts. These routes officially terminate at the get-on point for the lifts, but the route ahead continues unabated and develops into a track cut into the hillside, which corresponds to the Chemin du Pâtre blue.

This onward descent provides novices with the easiest route through this steeper terrain, sweeping wide to the right on a road-like track which takes a tight hairpin bend to the right, reversing direction and traversing across the line of the principal slopes again. The Chemin du Pâtre winds its way down the slopes in this fashion to take the line of least resistance, eventually linking with the base of the TSD Le Villarais chair lift, situated on the lower right. There is plenty of opportunity to drop off the lip of the track to take the wide and manageable central pistes down to the base area too, located at the bottom of the nearby short Tortue and Langaret button lifts which serve the gentler beginners' slopes below.

VILLARD

Below the get-on level for the Petit Prince button lifts, this is the widest, most direct descent on the central slopes. The Chemin du Pâtre blue cuts across the fall-line at least a couple of times – keep alert for crossing traffic.

The Villard is definitely the sector's best red, often with extensive mogul fields; it veers across the slope towards and under the line of the TSD Le Villarais chair lift, resulting in a testing right-to-left camber underfoot. Once on the far side of the chair lift line, you are joined from above right by La Forêt black. There is a choice of routes to finish: veer left under the line of the chair lift to merge with the Chemin du Pâtre blue, straight towards the chair lift base; or, to finish with more of a flourish, veer to the right into the steep chutes in the trees. This latter option takes you below the chair lift base, but delivers you to the main car park which has an unusual inclined-rail elevator to take you up to the chair lift.

LA FORÊT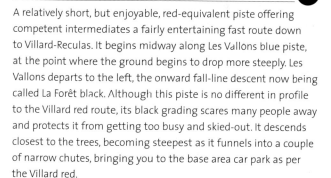

A relatively short, but enjoyable, red-equivalent piste offering competent intermediates a fairly entertaining fast route down to Villard-Reculas. It begins midway along Les Vallons blue piste, at the point where the ground begins to drop more steeply. Les Vallons departs to the left, the onward fall-line descent now being called La Forêt black. Although this piste is no different in profile to the Villard red route, its black grading scares many people away and protects it from getting too busy and skied-out. It descends closest to the trees, becoming steepest as it funnels into a couple of narrow chutes, bringing you to the base area car park as per the Villard red.

VILLARD-RECULAS 1480

A sleepy little mountain village, which is also the closest satellite ski station to Alpe d'Huez. It is perched halfway up the western flanks of le Signal de la Grande Sure, above the small town of Allemont in the Vallée de l'Eau d'Olle. Its balcony-like position on the mountainside endows it with sweeping views over the surrounding valleys, with the peaks of the Chaîne de Belledonne as a backdrop. The village consists of a small knot of farmhouses and barns, huddled around the local church, plus a scattering of chalets on the surrounding terraced hillside; with just three quiet bars/restaurants and a couple of equipment hire shops.

Access to the ski area is just above the entrance to the village (first left if arriving here on the road from Allemont). This simple base area has a plain roadside base lodge and a small open car park (located a little further along the road). The base lodge is a small

○ *Villard-Reculas village slopes, below La Bergerie mountain restaurant*

block of private apartments with a well-stocked convenience store and a small café/restaurant on the ground floor; it also houses the Villard-Reculas tourist office, a ski pass sales kiosk and WCs.

The Cloudit button lift rises from the lowest slopes just above the roadside, a little way past the base lodge, linking with the main lifts and ski area above; a very limited short beginners' slope is tucked away to the left of the Cloudit and is served by the Escargot rope tow. At the end of the road, an unusual little elevator (resembling a telephone cabin) departs from a hut at the car park and runs on an inclined rail, arriving just beside the base of the TSD Le Villarais chair lift.

There are two parallel-running button lifts serving the open lower slopes: the short left-hand lift is called the Tortue, the longer right-hand one is the Langaret. The lower slopes are a wide confluence finish area for all the main pistes descending from the Signal. However, there are an additional two named pistes served by, and running next to, the button lifts: the Chevreaux green piste descends to the right of the lifts and the Brebis blue piste descends to the left of them. The attractive La Bergerie restaurant is the only on-mountain venue in the Villard area, it is sited on the higher ground above the base area and is reachable on-piste close to the top of the Tortue button lift.

The TSD Le Villarais chair lift is the sole link lift out of the base area, rising to the summit of the Signal to reach Alpe d'Huez.

FURTHER INFORMATION
Villard-Reculas tourist information office:
📞 +33 (0)4 76 80 45 69   🌐 www.villard-reculas.com

LANGARET BUTTON LIFT

3 mins

- 153 m (502 ft) vertical rise
- 594 m (650 yd) long
- 900 passengers/hour

The longest of the two button lifts which run side-by-side up the lower slopes at Villard-Reculas base. The uppermost section is quite steep but manageable by progressing novices. On arrival, turn left for the Chevreaux green piste and the La Bergerie restaurant or the TSD Le Villarais chair lift; or, turn right for the Brebis blue.

The shorter Tortue button lift to the left serves the gentlest lower section of the Chevreaux piste and can also be used to reach the restaurant and the chair lift.

CHEVREAUX

Starting from the top of the Langaret button lift, but its gentlest lower section is served by the shorter Tortue button lift. This is the piste to progress to once you've exhausted Villard's limited beginners' zone. The piste is really a short blue, down past La Bergerie restaurant and back to the base of the button lifts. When conditions allow, you can get to the base of the Cloudit button lift to return to the village. Check your speed and your control as you approach the end of the slopes, as there's a sheer drop-off to the road below!

BREBIS

A tougher twin of the Chevreaux piste, on the opposite side of the Langaret button lift. It shares the slopes with the end section of the Souveraine red and also has a mild red profile. The route down is simply parallel to the lift line, back to the get-on level again.

TSD LE VILLARAIS CHAIR LIFT

7½ mins

- 546 m (1791 ft) vertical rise
- 1864 m (2039 yd) long
- 2000 passengers/hour

The sole link lift out of Villard-Reculas, to the summit of the Signal and linking with Alpe d'Huez. The lift is easily reached by descending to the right-hand side of the lower slopes if you are already on the mountain, or by using the funicular elevator from the car park when arriving from the village. There is a tool point at the get-on area and a piste map and information board just ahead to the right.

The journey up gives a bird's-eye view of all the pistes flowing down this side of the Signal, allowing you to get your bearings and giving you a chance to plan lines of descent. On arrival, U-turn back down the lift line for the Petit Prince and Les Vallons blues and La Forêt black back towards Villard; go straight ahead to link towards Alpe d'Huez's Rond Point des Pistes area via the Hirondelles blue piste; or, go ahead right for Le Signal restaurant and to link towards Alpe d'Huez via all other routes on the face of the Signal.

PETIT PRINCE BUTTON LIFTS

 5 mins

- 244 m (801 ft) vertical rise
- 1150 m (1258 yd) long

Two parallel-running lifts that serve the upper slopes at Villard-Reculas and rise to the summit of the Signal. The get-on area is only accessible via the mid section of the Souveraine red piste or from the Petit Prince and Les Vallons blues. Take the left-hand lift to ski the Petit Prince, Les Vallons or La Forêt pistes, the right-hand one for the Souveraine and Coqs reds or towards Alpe d'Huez.

VAUJANY / OZ SKI SECTOR

Fanning out over the northern margins of the Grandes Rousses domain, this extensive and diverse sector focuses on two satellite stations: the purpose-built Oz-en-Oisans Station (see page 184) and the attractive village of Vaujany; both are lift- and piste-linked into the core ski area. The compact satellite ski area of Montfrais 1650, furthest north in the domain, serves as base area for Vaujany, which interconnects with Oz on a sunny plateau at l'Alpette 2050. Both stations offer good cruising on varied terrain and their slopes are normally much quieter than the busy core ski area.

VAUJANY 1250

A proper working community, with true Oisans character, nestling in a peaceful side valley at the northern extremity of the Grandes Rousses. At a relatively modest 1250 m (4100 ft), it is the lowest altitude station in the domain, sited on the 'wrong' side of the valley, physically separated from the pistes. On paper, it doesn't have any of the accepted prerequisites of a successful ski station yet this classy little village has, by a quirk of fate and through spirited vision, managed to evolve into a fully-fledged micro-resort.

When the French national power authority decided to build a huge hydroelectric project in this vicinity, the citizens of Vaujany received a sizeable compensatory package. Consequently, the local council found themselves in the enviable position of having the means to build modern leisure facilities and fund ambitious projects to secure the viability of their otherwise marginal community. This also permitted them the luxury of improving their infrastructure whilst preserving the traditional charm of the village.

◀ *Beginning La Fare black run towards Vaujany*

A far-sighted idea to link Vaujany directly into the Grandes Rousses ski domain, using two of the largest and fastest cable cars in Europe, saved the village from rural obscurity and has established it as an important and alluring alternative to busier and brasher Alpe d'Huez. The massive Vaujany-Alpette cable car departs from the lower village centre and rises to an intermediate station at l'Alpette 2050, from where it is possible to make on-piste links towards either Oz or Montfrais or to link with the further Alpette-Rousses cable car to continue into the core Alpe d'Huez sectors via the summit of the Dôme des Petites Rousses.

The tiny base area of l'Enversin d'Oz is tucked away down on the valley floor beneath the village. It has a limited but pleasant beginners' zone and marks the finish area for Vaujany's 'home run' pistes. It is connected to the village by the Vaujany-Enversin gondola lift, which liaises with the central lift station at the main cable car. This lifts' hub is based around a wide metal-grid platform: it serves as the central ski schools' meeting point and houses an information desk, ski school office and ski pass sales kiosk. Another gondola lift, the Vaujany-Villette, also shares this hub, and runs further up the valley towards the hamlet of La Villette and the satellite ski area of Montfrais 1650. All these lifts are two-way and complete the circuit between Vaujany and its surrounding ski areas.

⬤ *The heart of Vaujany village*

Vaujany is built on a terraced hillside, facing directly across the valley towards the peaceful wooded flanks of the Dôme des Petites Rousses and le Signal de la Grande Sure, in the shadow of the rugged Pic de l'Etendard and Pic Blanc. The village has two distinct focal points: a pleasant little roadside square immediately above the lifts station; and a small commercial plaza in the uppermost residential area. There are several good restaurants and bars; a number of regional products shops and a patisserie; and a supermarket, tobacconist/newsagent and a couple of small boutiques. High quality, well-equipped ski hire shops are based in both the upper and lower areas. Leisure facilities include a natural ice rink, swimming pool and sports centre; a patrimony museum and a centre for the study of regional mountain fauna also provide a chance to engage with the human and natural history of this interesting community.

Although this is still a restful mountain hamlet at heart, the resort's few friendly bars and quality restaurants can become quite animated in the evenings and there are even a couple of small late-night music bars for those who still crave a more social experience.

Vaujany is best suited to those who rate the quality and style of the holiday as highly as the quality and extent of the ski area; particularly for those who seek a more authentic French ambiance. It also boasts one of the best-equipped crèches in the region, making it an excellent choice for discerning, ski-loving families.

FURTHER INFORMATION

Vaujany tourist information office:

📞 +33 (0)4 76 80 72 37   🌐 www.vaujany.com

VAUJANY-VILLETTE / VILLETTE-MONTFRAIS GONDOLA LIFT

 4³/4 mins +
5¹/4 mins

- 57 m (187 ft) + 367 m (1204 ft) vertical rise
- 963 m (1054 yd) + 820 m (897 yd) long
- 1500 passengers/hour

Departing from the far left-hand edge of the Vaujany lifts' hub platform, the Vaujany-Villette gondola lift travels almost horizontally up the valley to a mid-station a few hundred metres walk from the hamlet of La Villette, at a point which is currently the base of the Vaujaniate blue piste. The gondola cabins declutch within the station, allowing passengers to alight or board more easily, the mechanism turns selected cabins within the station for the return journey to Vaujany. However, you can also choose to remain in the same cabin to continue the journey on the line of the Villette-Montfrais section – taking 1½ minutes to pass through

the station. This second part of the journey rises steeply up to the Montfrais 1650 ski area, arriving at an upper station just a short stroll or skate from the cluster of lifts which serve the slopes above. Stepping down off the arrival platform, turn immediately to the right for the Montfrais button lifts; or, go ahead right for the Montfrais and Vallonnet chair lifts and Au P'tit Truc snack bar; the Vaujaniate blue piste begins ahead left.

MONTFRAIS 1650

This little cluster of lifts, pistes and mountain restaurants marks the northern-most boundary of the ski domain and serves as a satellite base area for Vaujany and La Villette. It can be reached using the Vaujany-Villette / Villette-Montfrais gondola lift (see opposite), or on-piste via the Chalets and Les Travers blue runs (see page 173) from l'Alpette 2050. Being at the outer limits of the ski domain, this area has a wilder and more marginal feel to it, yet has a welcoming and sheltered atmosphere where families and nervous novices can relax, away from the crowds. The surrounding scenery is quite unspoilt and the compact ski area is spread over undulating terrain beneath the highest peak in the Grandes Rousses, the rugged Pic de l'Etendard; with young fir trees peppering the mountainside and softening the otherwise bare rocky slopes.

The layout is quite simple: all the lifts are clustered together in the area beside the gondola lift station, with almost all pistes also flowing back to this point. The ski school classes meeting points are just next to the gondola lift platform, beside a piste patrol/first-aid cabin. Looking up the slopes from this level, the gondola lift platform is furthest right, the parallel-running Montfrais I and II button lifts depart immediately next to it and the Écureuils green piste and Étourneaux blue piste flow side-by-side back down beside the button lifts. The get-on point for the centrally located Montfrais chair lift is then just to the left of these pistes. To the far left, there is a tiny, plain snack bar called Au P'tit Truc, above and behind this is the get-on point for the Vallonnet chair lift; the Vaujaniate blue run slips out of the area from the lower left. The two main piste-side restaurants are located higher on the hillside above right, as is the area's small Snow Park.

MONTFRAIS I BUTTON LIFT

2³/₄ mins

- 53 m (174 ft) vertical rise
- 385 m (421 yd) long
- 720 passengers/hour

One of two parallel-running lifts departing from just above the gondola lift platform structure, providing uplift into the heart of this area around two restaurants above. Beginners should ensure that they get on this left-hand lift, since the Montfrais II lift to the right is a difficult lift and accesses terrain that is more testing.

The journey up allows you to view the slope that you will be descending on – the Écureuils green piste immediately to the left of the lift line. On arrival at the top, U-turn left on the track leading out to the start of the Écureuils piste towards Les Airelles mountain bar/restaurant.

ÉCUREUILS

The focus of all beginners' activity here at Montfrais, although the piste is really just the lower section of the Myrtilles blue run, rather than a distinct true green piste, and it is not ideal for absolute beginners.

Beginning as a track, leading away from the arrival point of the Montfrais I button lift, the piste then widens out at the point where it is joined from above right by traffic coming from the Snow Park and Myrtilles and Les Travers blues; the attractive Les Airelles bar/restaurant is just below, its terraces spilling out on to the left-hand side of the piste. Continuing past the restaurant, the piste then runs down past Le Vaujaniat self-service restaurant towards the lifts base again; the piste sharing the slope to the right is the Étourneaux blue.

VAUJANIATE

Flowing away from the base of the lifts at Montfrais 1650 and serving almost as a home run for the sleepy hamlet of La Villette. It starts gently, but quickly develops into a good fast blue, slicing across the mountainside as a well-maintained motorway; joined from above right by the Roche Melon black.

The Glacier de Barbarate is high above this area and the melt-water flows down the craggy flanks on your right, frequently producing fabulous blue ice flows at this side of the piste.

The run is normally quiet, with very light traffic, inviting a fast cruise along the uppermost straight before turning sharply to the left, working your edges hard to tackle a series of sweeping bends on the steeper slopes beyond. After piste-marker six, the route peters out and traverses gently through quiet woods along the valley towards the gondola lift mid-station, needing a skate in soft conditions. The hamlet of La Villette can be reached by walking along the track leaving to the right, otherwise continue straight ahead towards the lift.

At the lift station, the steps nearest on the left of the platform lead up to the cabins heading back up to Montfrais 1650; for Vaujany, walk to the right and go under the platform and up the steps on the far side.

From 2007, there will be an extension to this route which will continue down the valley to l'Enversin d'Oz.

🔺 *Blue ice flows at the side of the Vaujaniate blue piste*

VALLONNET CHAIR LIFT

8³/4 mins	• 377 m (1237 ft) vertical rise • 1120 m (1225 yd) long • 1500 passengers/hour

Departing from just above and behind Au P'tit Truc snack bar; the piste ending here to the left is the Edelweiss blue. This older chair has a vicious kick at the get-on point, so prepare for it and grab the frame to ease yourself on. The journey up gives good views over the Montfrais 1650 area; this is the outermost lift at this limit of the ski domain and the Edelweiss blue and Roche Melon black are the only pistes out to the left; the rest of the upper valley towards the Col du Couard is wild and untouched. On arrival, there is a short dip down an off-ramp after dismounting; turn left for all routes.

EDELWEISS

This tough blue should really only be tackled by those who are at least of a very competent novice standard; it is too severe for absolute beginners. From the top of the Vallonnet chair lift, it starts off fairly steeply and then turns tightly to the left to funnel into a narrow track; the Roche Melon black branches off to the right. The route then picks its way down the rocky slopes in a series of twisting bends before dropping more directly for the steepest section of the run; there is a less steep escape track cut out to the right of the piste at this point for more cautious visitors. The final straight flattens out and veers left towards the lifts; you can also continue the descent by keeping to the right and passing behind the snack bar to link with the Vaujaniate blue run below.

ROCHE MELON

A seldom open piste which marks the northern limit of the Grandes Rousses domain, accessed using the Vallonnet chair lift and the uppermost section of the Edelweiss blue piste. When open, this run is definitely worth a blast, for the novelty of riding at the edge of the ski area and because the steep and rocky slope here gives a very good workout. The entrance is off the right-hand side of the upper Edelweiss piste and the route is basically a direct fall-line version of that blue-graded neighbour. The boulder-strewn inter-piste terrain, amongst well-scattered stunted trees is very inviting for advanced riders, but do take care as there are a lot of hidden rocks and potholes on these jagged scree slopes.

The lower section of the run maintains a good steep descent, eventually finishing by dropping down to join the Vaujaniate blue piste.

● Looking up the Vaujaniate piste, from the finish of the Roche Melon run

MONTFRAIS CHAIR LIFT

4

5³/₄ mins

- 252 m (827 ft) vertical rise
- 730 m (799 yd) long
- 1500 passengers/hour

The central lift at Montfrais 1650, accessing its greatest variety of pistes, including the Snow Park. The journey up gives you a good opportunity to study the area's layout and plan your descent. On arrival, turn left for the Grand Combe and La Stade reds; or, turn right for the Éteaux and Étourneaux blues. The Éteaux route will link you with the Clos Giraud chair lift towards l'Alpette 2050.

GRAND COMBE / LA STADE

Beginning together at the top of the Montfrais chair lift, these are basically twins which flow as fast corduroy-snow ribbons down the otherwise gnarled and rocky slopes. From the shared start section, La Stade peels off to the left; it is the area's competition course and is often closed for events and local ski-club training sessions. The Grand Combe ranges further out to the right, heading towards the line of the Vallonnet chair lift and eventually merges into the Edelweiss blue piste for the final approach to this lift.

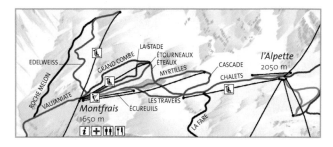

ÉTOURNEAUX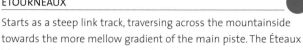

Starts as a steep link track, traversing across the mountainside towards the more mellow gradient of the main piste. The Éteaux blue also shares this uppermost link section, but continues straight ahead past the point where the Étourneaux turns down to the right. The Étourneaux then widens considerably and develops into a good high-end blue, with a profile very similar to that of La Stade red competition course, with some lovely kickers and boulder drop-offs amongst the well-spaced small trees at the sides. The piste flows directly down the middle of the slopes, passing the restaurants level to merge with the Écureuils green piste below for the final approach to the lifts base: at the bottom, turn left for the Montfrais button lifts or the gondola upper station; or, turn right for all other lifts and to link with the Vaujaniate blue run.

ÉTEAUX

Sharing an initial steep track with the Étourneaux blue, the Éteaux serves as a link from the top of the Montfrais chair lift over to the Clos Giraud chair lift, allowing you to leave the Montfrais 1650 area and head towards the sectors' interchange at l'Alpette 2050. After the Étourneaux piste swoops away down to the right, the Éteaux continues straight ahead to traverse the mountainside as a gentle road-like track; take care ahead as the route crosses over the Myrtilles piste as well as the line of the Montfrais II button lift. The route finally exits out at a confluence point with the Cascade and Les Travers pistes, crossing Les Travers blue to reach the lift on the far side of this piste. The Éteaux is also handy for accessing the Montfrais Snow Park, reached by joining the Myrtilles piste.

MONTFRAIS II BUTTON LIFT

8 mins

- 159 m (522 ft) vertical rise
- 833 m (911 yd) long
- 900 passengers/hour

The get-on point for this lift is situated alongside the shorter Montfrais I button lift, right beside the rear of the gondola lift platform. Take care at the get-on point as the lift jolts when the declutchable lift-poles reconnect with the haul cable. The first section of the journey mirrors that of the slower Montfrais I lift which is running parallel on the left; just after the Montfrais I ends, the journey then takes you across the line of Les Travers blue piste, which is entering the Montfrais area from the right – traffic should be looking out for you, but stay alert. After the next much steeper section, the lift line veers to the left and the ground dips away down a short slope. You then cross over the route of the Éteaux link piste, its traffic coming at you from the left – again, remain alert. The final section of the lift is quite jerky as the cables travel over the pylon mechanisms. The dismount area is wide and easy, with a slight dip away from the lift: turn right for the Cascade blue or left for the Myrtilles blue.

The views from this higher altitude are worth pausing for; looking over the entire Montfrais area and sweeping down the valley to the peaks of the Chaîne de Belledonne on the horizon.

🔺 *The peaks of the Chaîne de Belledonne, viewed from the upper Montfrais slopes*

MYRTILLES

A good, wide blue, with a fairly consistent fall-line profile all the way from its start point at the top of the Montfrais II button lift. After providing a good warm-up on the uppermost section, the run is then crossed by the route of the Éteaux link track; as long as this is free of traffic you should experience no let-up. The Montfrais Snow Park is on the right just below this crossing area. The main piste continues to the left of the park and maintains its pace heading towards the point where Les Travers blue piste links in to the Montfrais area from the left. Both routes finish together by converging with the Écureuils green piste, which continues the descent past the piste-side restaurants and down to the lifts base below.

SNOW PARK

The Montfrais Snow Park is quite small, with no halfpipe and a limited range of modules, however, it is very easy to get to and is almost perfect for beginners and progressing novices and provides a relatively good in-line run. It is situated on the right-hand side of the Myrtilles blue piste and is accessed either from that piste, using the Montfrais II button lift, or via the Éteaux blue link route, using the Montfrais chair lift. The park is also conveniently close to Les Airelles restaurant, located piste-side on the Écureuils green piste which provides the short and easy return to the lifts base.

MODULES

- Flat rail
- Flat/flat-down rail
- Simple quarter
- Various kickers and tabletops

CASCADE

A simple link route across the mountainside from the top of the Montfrais II button lift to connect with the Clos Giraud chair lift towards the sectors' interchange at l'Alpette 2050. Take care at the finish area because the route converges with the Éteaux link route and crosses the busier Les Travers piste to reach the chair lift.

CLOS GIRAUD CHAIR LIFT

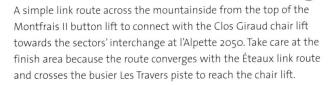

11³/₄ mins

- 234 m (768 ft) vertical rise
- 1521 m (1664 yd) long
- 1500 passengers/hour

The handiest link out of the Montfrais area to reach the major lifts and sectors' interchange at l'Alpette 2050; make sure that you take this lift by 16.00 hours at the latest if you want to return towards Alpe d'Huez before the link-lifts close. The lift is reached using either the Éteaux or Cascade blue link routes and is located at the left-hand side of the Chalets blue piste coming from l'Alpette 2050, at the point where this piste becomes Les Travers blue linking towards Montfrais 1650. The final approach to the lift is via a narrow track; the control gates are on the right-hand side.

The journey up is slow but, on a clear day, affords great views towards Vaujany and over the Lac du Verney.

On arrival, go straight off the lift and veer left for all onward links; watch out for traffic coming off the nearby button lift. The huge lift station structure here is the mid-station for the Vaujany cable cars; the upper Alpette-Rousses cabin links with the core Alpe d'Huez Mid sector.

❶ The Clos Giraud non-declutchable chair lift will be upgraded to a declutchable chair lift in 2007.

CHALETS / LES TRAVERS

The Chalets piste departs from the wide plateau at l'Alpette 2050, to the right of the huge cable cars mid-station; it provides the sole on-piste link towards the Montfrais 1650 area, via the further Les Travers piste, and accesses the enjoyable La Fare black run towards Vaujany.

The right-hand side of the Chalets piste is graded green. Beginners can use the Lamat button lift parallel to the right to return to the main plateau; once below the get-on level of the Lamat lift you are committed on the Chalets run all the way down to the Clos Giraud chair lift before you can return to l'Alpette 2050.

The Chalets is a standard wide blue, providing an easy cruise; more experienced visitors can spice things up by riding off from the right-hand side of the piste into some great freeride terrain; full of natural kickers and quarters, stream gullies and boulder drop-offs, weaving around well-scattered small trees, all within easy reach of the piste to maintain the onward links. The piste itself gradually becomes even more mellow in gradient towards a wide junction point: La Fare black run departs to the left; keep straight on, highest right, to reach the Clos Giraud chair lift or to continue towards Montfrais 1650. Nearing the Clos Giraud lift, the Cascade and Éteaux link routes cross from the right to reach the lift on the left-hand side of this piste; from this point on, the Chalets becomes Les Travers, continuing towards the Montfrais area, initially as a gentle track then dropping away on a steeper straight for around 400 m (438 yd). The route then swings round to the right to carefully converge with the Montfrais area's Myrtilles blue piste: veer down to the left, passing Les Airelles piste-side restaurant, to reach the Montfrais 1650 lifts base via the Écureuils green piste.

LA FARE

Accessed via the Chalets blue piste from l'Alpette 2050. This long run is nowhere near a true black, but is definitely worth the effort for an enjoyable cruise and good workout on its at least fair red-equivalent route, with the added bonus that the black grading scares most people away to leave this run quiet and open for a fast blast. There is usually an information board placed in the middle of the junction from the Chalets piste, informing you about the time of the last lift link towards Alpe d'Huez: if you don't reckon you'll reach the lifts in time, simply traverse over to rejoin the Chalets piste and take the closer Clos Giraud chair lift back up to l'Alpette 2050 for return links.

La Fare begins by sweeping round to the left, under the line of the Clos Giraud chair lift, immediately developing a decent red-profile gradient on a well-maintained, standard width piste; with great views straight down the valley towards the Lac du Verney and the town of Allemont. The route has some fast twists and turns, but also a couple of long gentle blue-equivalent straights, passing under the line of the Vaujany-Alpette cable car. The surroundings are very peaceful, adding to the appeal of this run, with only birdsong and the gentle distant hum of the lifts rising above the silence.

Nearing the valley floor, you come to a junction point which marks the end of La Fare. To the left is the short Combe Bénite red run, which maintains a consistent and steeper finish down to a button lift of the same name, linking to the Vaujany-Enversin gondola lift towards Vaujany. Continuing down to the right, the main route becomes the Fontbelle blue piste, indistinguishable from La Fare at this point and maintaining a fair pace to link well with the Vaujany-Enversin gondola lift.

L'ENVERSIN D'OZ

A peaceful little dell at the lower station of the Vaujany-Enversin gondola lift, serving as Vaujany village beginners' zone/sledging hill and marking the end of the home-run pistes. The area's sole, short green-graded slope (the Sapins) is served by the Combe Bénite button lift, linking with the Vaujany-Enversin gondola lift to return to Vaujany.

VAUJANY-ENVERSIN GONDOLA LIFT

5 mins ▲▼

- 113 m (371 ft) vertical rise
- 610 m (667 yd) long
- 675 passengers/hour

Used both for reaching l'Enversin d'Oz from Vaujany and for reaching Vaujany lifts hub and village if travelling from La Fare piste.

While in the station, stay well away from the edge of the platform. The cabins are grouped in clusters of three and the lift runs using the Pulse system, alternately speeding up and slowing down as each cluster travels through the stations. The cabins have no seating, but have a central pole to hold on to; the perspex sidewalls let in plenty of natural light and make the most of the views.

On arrival at Vaujany, step out onto the wide platform: all other lifts are to the right on this same level, as is a tourist office. Stairs, an escalator and a lift are at the far side of the platform, leading towards the patrimony centre and village square (see page 161).

VAUJANY-ALPETTE CABLE CAR

7½ mins ▲▼

- 812 m (2664 ft) vertical rise
- 2464 m (2696 yd) long
- 1400 passengers/hour

A huge, state-of-art cable car which, when combined with its twin (the Alpette-Rousses lift onward from l'Alpette 2050), links Vaujany to the core Alpe d'Huez Mid sector almost as swiftly as is possible from Alpe d'Huez itself. This enormous project was funded by the massive injection of funds that the community of Vaujany received as compensation when the French national power authority constructed a hydroelectric dam in the vicinity, inundating a considerable area of farmland and dwellings.

The lift's base station at Vaujany village sits just below the level of the main road, next to the central square, and shares a wide platform with the two other lifts which connect the village with the surrounding ski area. Keep clear of the sidewall barriers at the boarding area, because these are hydraulically mobile and slowly drop horizontally to create a bridge to the lift cabin once it is in the station. Average loading time is around 4½ minutes.

The journey up affords fantastic views and travels at a dizzying height across the valley; the piste winding its way down the wooded slopes ahead is La Fare black (see page 174).

On arrival, exit straight off the platform into the station, from here you then have two choices: either exit via the wide steps down to the right to step out on to the plateau at l'Alpette 2050, to make onward links with Oz-en-Oisans Station or Montfrais 1650; or, remain in the station building and simply stroll straight ahead on this same level to the adjacent control gates for the second half of the ascent towards the Alpe d'Huez sectors, via the Alpette-Rousses cable car.

ALPETTE-ROUSSES CABLE CAR

5½ mins

- 755 m (2477 ft) vertical rise
- 1644 m (1799 yd) long
- 1780 passengers/hour

A massive lift, the second half of the link from Vaujany into the upper Alpe d'Huez sectors, provides an efficient link from the busy l'Alpette 2050 interchange. If you're joining from l'Alpette 2050, keep to the right up the steps into the building to stay clear of traffic exiting from the Vaujany-Alpette. Once inside, the Vaujany-Alpette cabin is on the left and the upward Alpette-Rousses cabin is to the right; a traffic light system controls queues on to the lift platform. Keep clear of the sidewall barriers at the boarding area – these are hydraulically mobile and slowly drop horizontally to create a bridge to the lift cabin once it's in the station. Average loading time is around 4½ minutes.

The journey up rises steeply over the sheer cliffs of the Dôme des Petites Rousses. On arrival, walk straight off the platform and along the catwalk to reach the start of Le Dôme and Le Belvédère red pistes. This arrival station itself is a stunning piece of engineering, cantilevered over a precipice, the vertigo-inducing drop beneath your feet visible through the metal platform grid.

⬤ *Alpette-Rousses cable car upper station*

LE DÔME / LE BELVÉDÈRE / DOLOMITS

Three spliced pistes that link routes from the arrival point of the Alpette-Rousses cable car, from the summit of Le Dôme des Petites Rousses, towards the major 2700 area interchange above Alpe d'Huez. From the catwalk at the cable car arrival platform, you step on to the flattened dome of the summit, needing a further short stroll or skate to reach any useful gradient. There is a piste patrol/first-aid hut to the left on the summit, along with an avalanche risk notice board. Alpe d'Huez lies down to the right; Pic Blanc is above left, its cable car visible on clear days rising up to the summit station. The exposed off-piste Agnelin route drops off the summit close to the cliffs roped-off on the right: employ a mountain guide to discover this and other advanced tours in the domain (see page 77).

Le Dôme is the most direct and fastest piste ahead left, eventually dropping with a respectably steep slope angle for around 200-250 m (219–274 yd), giving a good warm-up after the static period in the lift; Le Belvédère is a mellower twin out to the right. Both pistes rejoin further below and are then joined/crossed from the left by an exit track from the black pistes coming from the Pic Blanc Tunnel. At this point there is a choice of onward routes: Le Dôme and Le Belvédère turn right and become a single long contour-hugging flat track, along with the Tunnel pistes traffic, towards the 2700 area interchange – rideable but no fun; alternatively, continuing straight down from Le Dôme and Le Belvédère begins the much more enjoyable Dolomits red, which is a direct continuation of the same pisted slopes that steepen further to provide a good fast workout straight down to the base of the Lac Blanc chair lift, again linking to the 2700 area interchange.

LAC BLANC CHAIR LIFT

2¹/₄ mins

- 104 m (341 ft) vertical rise
- 245 m (268 yd) long
- 2000 passengers/hour

This link-lift permits a more enjoyable end to the Dôme des Petites Roussés and Pic Blanc Tunnel runs; because it is based down in the Lac Blanc tarn depression you can prolong your run down to this lower level rather than having to skate over the flatter, higher ground above to reach the 2700 area interchange for onward links.

The lift arrives on a hillock above the 2700 area interchange. On arrival, move swiftly away from the dismount area – if you need to clip into bindings, step off to the right to keep clear of traffic. The easy link track flows down to the left to emerge next to the Grotte de Glace (ice cave) in front of the Pic Blanc cable car station; turn right here to start Les Rousses red down to l'Alpette 2050 and towards Oz-en-Oisans Station; or, veer left to access the cable car station, shared with the arriving Grandes Rousses (DMC) cable car, and to start the Couloir blue and Chamois red pistes into the core Alpe d'Huez sectors.

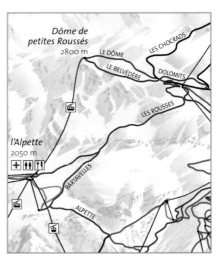

LES ROUSSES / BARTAVELLES

Les Rousses is the sole on-piste route towards Vaujany from the core Alpe d'Huez sectors. Although graded as a red, it has an easier alternative entrance which makes it manageable for competent novices too. The Bartavelles piste is a similar, lower section, variation linking into the Oz-en-Oisans ski area.

There are three entrances to Les Rousses: the highest begins just to the left of the Grotte de Glace, behind the 2700 area cable car station; the second and third are accessed via the Chamois and Couloir pistes – the third, lowest, entrance being the easiest. Only the uppermost variation qualifies as a true red, eventually merging with the second similar profile variant to drop down onto the lowermost easy track. There is also a steep off-piste chute to keep more experienced visitors entertained, beginning just off to the right at the point where the first and second sections converge.

After merging together, all variations then swing to the right across the mountainside as a wide cruise, with a long and flat mid-section funnelling through a cutting before building any real pace. The slope angle steepens best as you approach l'Alpette 2050, with a choice of two onward routes: either keep to the right to continue on Les Rousses, zooming down across the plateau below; or, veer left to head towards Oz-en-Oisans as the Bartavelles. The Bartavelles still allows you to reach l'Alpette 2050, by linking with the short Alpette button lift; if you don't need to reach l'Alpette quickly, then this is definitely the best option. The Bartavelles glides past the piste-side Auberge de l'Alpette restaurant to converge with the Carrelet green piste towards the button lift; or, you can swing left to continue the descent towards Oz-en-Oisans via the Alpette red route (see page 183).

L'ALPETTE 2050

This wide and frequently sunny plateau, beneath the cliffs of the Dôme des Petites Rousses, is a key interchange between Alpe d'Huez and the Vaujany/Oz sector. The only piste linking into the area is Les Rousses red (see opposite); this is easy enough to make it a viable option for competent novices. The Boucle des Lac Nordic circuit also extends this far, from the 2100 area in Alpe d'Huez's main Town sector; fit walkers can follow the same route.

The area is served by no fewer than three mountain restaurants (see pages 229–30) and has a small sledging slope and a children's Snow Garden. Although a busy junction, the plateau is still a lot less hectic than the core Alpe d'Huez sectors.

The main focal point is the huge Vaujany cable cars mid-station, which is surrounded by a cluster of further lift arrival points: the Clos Giraud chair lift arrives at the far side of the station, the Alpette gondola lift and Alpette button lift arrive directly in front.

Another short button lift, the Lamat, serves a wide green-graded slope near La Grange restaurant under the cliffs; the wide piste flowing off the plateau here too is the Chalets blue, leading towards Montfrais and Vaujany.

⬤ *The plateau at l'Alpette 2050*

CARRELET

A wide, easy cruise down the line of the Alpette gondola lift; good for beginners and nervous novices, and useful as a link route towards the Oz-en-Oisans ski area for more experienced visitors, with the added bonus of having an easy spur out to the left to reach the nearby piste-side Auberge de l'Alpette restaurant (see page 229). The piste veers to the right under the gondola lift line to finish at the get-on point for l'Alpette button lift.

L'ALPETTE BUTTON LIFT

3 mins

- 123 m (404 ft) vertical rise
- 618 m (676 yd) long
- 800 passengers/hour

Although specifically serving the Carrelet green piste, this relatively short drag lift also provides a handy link to the main plateau area at l'Alpette 2050 when coming from the Bartavelles red piste. Novices should note that this lift has a awkward jolt just after mounting and the final section is a little steeper. On arrival at the top, turn right and take care not to impede passengers arriving from the nearby Clos Giraud chair lift. The Vaujany cable cars mid-station is ahead right.

ALPETTE

Accessed via the Bartavelles red run from Alpe d'Huez's 2700 area interchange, or via the Carrelet green off the plateau at l'Alpette 2050. The gradient is quite respectable, making this a worthwhile link; the route is simply a road-like track which has been cut into the mountainside above Oz-en-Oisans Station, traversing almost straight across towards a joining point with the similar profile Champclotury blue route – check your speed when merging. The cliffs towering above left and the ground dropping away steeply to the right enhance the feeling of descending deep into the valley; Oz-en-Oisans Station is below right, with the Lac du Verney beyond.

The Alpette ends at the junction with the Champclotury blue, which joins from above left, simply keep straight on as a continuation of the descent; at this point, the Roche Noire black run drops off to the right, heading directly towards Oz-en-Oisans Station – it's best not to take this if you want to reach the Poutran I gondola lift, because the piste ends a walk away from it.

ROCHE NOIRE

The low altitude here takes its toll on this fairly steep, wide chute, down the wooded slopes directly above Oz-en-Oisans Station, and the run is frequently closed because of poor snow cover. When open, the run serves as this station's slalom course; it's really a fair-to-good red equivalent and is a relatively short 800 m (875 yd) long, so don't feel that you are missing out if it is closed.

At the bottom, turn right to join the link piste to reach the Alpette gondola station; the Poutran I gondola departs from the opposite side of this small satellite ski station, requiring a walk out to the left to reach it.

OZ-EN-OISANS STATION 1350

This small, purpose-built ski station has the distinction of being the closest Oisans resort to Grenoble, although it has nowhere near the regional draw of its larger, more glitzy neighbours. There is only one hotel, the rest of the accommodation is self-catering apartments and chalets; the pleasant low-key architecture is not invasive and the quiet, wooded surroundings are attractive and sheltered. The station sits at a relatively modest 1350 m (4428 ft), overlooking the Lac du Verney towards the peaks of the Chaîne de Belledonne. It is linked into the Grandes Rousses ski domain by two gondola lifts, located at the upper end of the resort within easy reach of all accommodation; they link into Alpe d'Huez's major 2100 area interchange and towards Vaujany via the interchange at l'Alpette 2050. There are several home run pistes, almost all of which are secured with snowmaking equipment. A separate, sheltered beginners' zone nestles amongst the trees in the lower Clos du Pré area of the resort and it is floodlit for night-skiing on a couple of evenings per week around major holiday periods. The slopes adjacent to the resort are being enlarged and developed further, with a beginners' Snow Park being constructed to open by 2007.

The station has a children's Snow Garden and organizes a regular weekly programme of entertainment, particularly aimed at families with young children: throughout the school holidays, the local ski school instructors put on a weekly show of torchlit synchronized skiing, with free *vin chaud* for spectators.

The setting has appeal for Nordic ski enthusiasts too, with a short, blue-graded circuit at resort level and direct access to the extensive, well-maintained Alpe d'Huez circuits at the top of the Poutran gondola lifts.

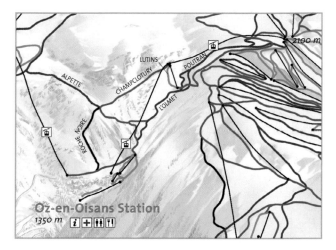

The resort has no central focus, but is compact enough not to need one; all accommodation is just a short stroll from all the lifts and facilities. There are several small bars and restaurants, a supermarket, tobacconist/newsagent, souvenir shop and a regional produce shop. Leisure facilities include an ice rink, a cinema, a sports hall and an indoor climbing wall.

Oz is perfect for families and couples seeking a break away from the crowds but wanting the option of access to an extensive ski area, with more charm than most larger purpose-built resorts.

FURTHER INFORMATION

Oz-en-Oisans tourist information office:

☏ +33 (0)4 76 80 78 01   🌐 www.oz-en-oisans.com

ALPETTE GONDOLA LIFT

 7 mins ▲▼
- 676 m (2218 ft) vertical rise
- 1950 m (2133 yd) long
- 1600 passengers/hour

At the upper left of Oz-en-Oisans Station, easily reached on foot and from the end of the home runs. The lift arrives at a lift interchange on the plateau at l'Alpette 2050: the Alpette-Rousses cable car is straight ahead (connects with the Pic Blanc cable car towards the Glacier de Sarenne and links into the core Alpe d'Huez Mid sector); turn right for all pistes (see page 181).

POUTRAN I & II GONDOLA LIFTS

  **7 mins +
4¹/₂ mins**
- 530 m (1739 ft) + 224 m (735 ft) vertical rise
- 1629 m (1782 yd) + 1109 m (1213 yd) long
- 2000 passengers/hour

At the upper right-hand corner of Oz-en-Oisans Station, at the base of the home-run pistes. The base station houses the tourist office, a ski pass kiosk, WCs and an indoor climbing wall; there is a piste patrol/first-aid cabin at the bottom of the access stairs.

The lift is in two-stages, via a mid-station at 1876 m (6153 ft):

Mid-station – exit to start the Champclotury blue and Lutins green pistes; this mid-station can also be reached using the Champ Clotury button lift from the Bld des Lutins blue piste.

Upper station – behind the Grandes Rousses (DMC) cable car station and Chantebise 2100 restaurant at the busy 2100 area interchange (see page 106); U-turn right on arrival to start the Poutran red run and the Bld des Lutins blue run; the Boucle de Poutran Nordic circuit and the main Alpe d'Huez beginners' zone are below right, the Boucle des Lacs Nordic circuit is on the far side of the main lift and restaurant buildings.

 Section of the Boucle de Poutran Nordic circuit

POUTRAN / L'OLMET

Starting from the busy 2100 area interchange: if you are skiing down into this area, it's easiest to go through the little tunnel under the arriving Jeux button lifts; from the top of the Poutran II gondola lift, the route starts right beside the lift station. This top section is very flat for the first 250 m (274 yd) or so before picking up a more respectable gradient, parallel to the gondola lift line; the gentler twin parallel to the left is the Bld des Lutins blue. The Bld des Lutins swings to the right as an easier, track-like route; the Poutran takes the steepest slope down to the left; both reconverge after just 200 m (219 yd) approaching the cosy Perce-Neige bar/restaurant (see page 228) and the base of the Champ Clotury button lift – used for accessing the mid-station of the Poutran gondola lift. From here the continuing descent is known as l'Olmet red run.

Le Croc' Neige bar/restaurant (see page 228) is further down on the right, nearing a junction point which offers an easier blue track out to right to join the Champclotury blue piste; keep ahead left for the final true red section, which also ends by joining the Champclotury blue for the final approach to Oz-en-Oisans Station.

CHAMP CLOTURY BUTTON LIFT

 | 2¼ mins | • 40 m (131 ft) vertical rise
• 169 m (185 yd) long
• 700 passengers/hour

A short drag lift providing uplift from just below the Perce-Neige bar/restaurant up to join the Poutran gondola lifts at their mid-station. Useful for avoiding the full descent to Oz-en-Oisans Station if snow conditions are poor below this point, or if you're worried about making the last lift back towards Alpe d'Huez.

LUTINS

Although graded as a green, this short piste is really a tough blue, nudging on red! It is not aimed at beginners and simply denotes an easy on-piste link from the mid station of the Poutran gondola lifts down to the Perce-Neige bar/restaurant, where you can join the red l'Olmet route down to Oz-en-Oisans Station.

CHAMPCLOTURY

Although beginning on its own at the mid-station level of the Poutran gondola lifts, this fairly gentle route is eventually joined by the other main pistes in this area to provide the home run to Oz-en-Oisans Station. The uppermost section, flowing away from the lift station, is an almost direct traverse across the mountainside, best avoided in late afternoon as the area is in deep shadow and, consequently, very icy underfoot and with poor visibility. Take care at the junction with the Alpette red run, joining at right angles from the right, as traffic is fast-moving and often unaware that the route converges at this point. From here, the Champclotury turns down to the left to lead the onward descent on the lower section of the road-like route of the now officially finished Alpette red. The route is also joined from above left by two variations of the l'Olmet red run; all merge and flow together for the final approach to Oz-en-Oisans Station. The gentle track veering off to the left is a link towards the lower Clos du Pré beginners' zone; keep straight ahead for the Poutran I gondola lift base station (also housing the tourist office, WCs and a piste patrol/first-aid point); or, turn right to follow the gentle track along the top of the resort to reach the Alpette gondola lift (towards l'Alpette 2050, Vaujany and Montfrais 1650).

AURIS SKI SECTOR

Compared with the other Grandes Rousses satellite stations, Auris offers by far the most extensive range of pistes and terrain; integrally complete as a little resort and ski in its own right. Its base station is a central focal point for the surrounding ski area, with a good selection of home runs.

The ski area is quite separate from that of Alpe d'Huez, sitting on the opposite side of the deep Gorge de Sarenne; the two-way Alpauris chair lift is the principal link, descending into then climbing out of the chasm that separates them. The resort is almost as close to Les Deux Alpes as it is to Alpe d'Huez, with great views over the upper Romanche valley towards this distant Oisans neighbour and the stunning, classically Alpine peak of La Meije beyond.

AURIS-EN-OISANS STATION 1600

This is the actual 'resort' and ski station, as opposed to Auris-en-Oisans village which is perched on the mid-altitude flanks of the valley, well below the ski area. At 1600 m (5248 ft), the station's altitude is sufficiently high to ensure that it is possible to ski to resort level throughout the season.

Auris markets itself as a family resort and makes an effort to offer the facilities and friendly atmosphere needed to ensure that children feel welcome. The resort is very popular with the French themselves, thus preserving the Gallic charm that attracts discerning visitors to such a small and relatively little-known ski station in the first instance. Being so close to Les Deux Alpes, and yet linked to Alpe d'Huez, means that the resort is an ideal choice for self-drive holidaymakers wishing to explore this region.

◀ Auris-en-Oisans 1600, approaching on the Col and Gentianes home runs

SKI AREA

The ski area is spread over three summits, in a semicircular arc above the resort. The Piegut area to the upper left is a sheltered, wooded hillside which serves as the main beginners area: it is accessed using the Piegut chair lift from the base station and offers novices a non-threatening environment in which to relax and enjoy the learning process. At the summit, there are two short button lifts and several genuinely green-grade slopes, safely tucked away from the main ski area. The open and undulating slopes flow gently back to the resort, with an attractive alternative route on a peaceful track through the nearby forest, passing the upper resort centre and finishing at the lower base level.

The lowermost slopes on this side of the ski area are served by a pair of parallel-running button lifts (the Bauchets). These are a bit too steep, and the adjacent slopes are a bit too busy, to make them ideal for absolute beginners, but they are handy for gaining height to reach the upper centre of the resort. Right next to this upper centre (place des Écrins) there is a small children's playground and two separate Snow Gardens, safely roped-off and monitored by the ESF ski school children's ski instructors (access by reservation only, see page 78 for further information).

Immediately above the resort, Les Sures summit offers an enjoyable range of more intermediate-level terrain, most manageable by competent novices, served directly from the base station by the Sures chair lift. The summit provides an excellent vantage point to get your bearings within the Grandes Rousses domain – taking in most of the Auris sector and extending over to Alpe d'Huez and the Pic Blanc massif.

A small Snow Park occupies the uppermost slopes at Les Sures and there are a couple of good blues sweeping back towards the base station. You can also drop down into the outermost margins of the domain at Le Châtelard, via one of the most severely mogulled black pistes in the area; although there are blue and red alternative routes as well.

The third sub-sector of Auris, and the link towards Alpe d'Huez, is accessed using the Auris Express chair lift out of the base area to arrive on the mid-altitude flanks of the Signal de l'Homme. This mountain is served by a collection of chair lifts and button lifts and offers Auris' best intermediate-level red pistes, on predominately north-facing snow-sure slopes. This area faces directly across to Alpe d'Huez and is linked to it by the Alpauris two-way chair lift; it is also possible to descend on-piste all the way to the valley floor in the Gorge de Sarenne to reach the Chalvet chair lift linking to the slopes above Alpe d'Huez's Bergers quarter. To return from Bergers, you must take the Alpauris chair lift, meaning there is only a red-graded link towards Auris.

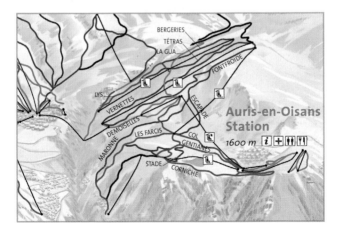

AURIS RESORT

The resort has two distinct focal centres: the lower place des Orgières, at the entrance to the station, beyond which lie the principal base-area pistes and lifts; and the upper place des Écrins, which serves as the 'village square' and heart of the resort.

The place des Orgières contains a small commercial centre, housing the tourist office, ski school office, ski pass sales kiosk, WCs, ATM, two equipment hire shops, snack bar/restaurant (Le Tetras) and a well-stocked supermarket, all on a mezzanine walkway, just above the resort's main free car park. Immediately behind this building, and accessible from it, are the base area slopes (including a separate sledging hill), ski school classes meeting points and ski lifts. They are all clustered within an easy stroll or skate from the ski pass sales kiosk. All major lifts fan out from this area to access the three summits which form the ski area, with home run pistes flowing back to this central point. A further building to the upper right houses the Post Office, which also trades as a newsagent/tobacconist, and a piste-side restaurant (La Bucherie).

The upper place des Écrins level is the social heart of the resort, with an open square surrounded by apartment buildings, small commercial units and a bar/restaurant, directly accessible from the pistes on the Piegut side of the ski area. The piste-side end of this square has a children's playground and is right next to the children's Snow Gardens. The central plaza contains a terrace bar/restaurant (L'Isba) and there are a couple of equipment rental shops, a small supermarket and a photographic studio.

Although not that large, and with few alternative leisure facilities, Auris is a great little resort. It has a real soul, offering an enticing alternative for both families and those wanting a more

○ *Place des Écrins, Auris-en-Oisans resort*

relaxed and authentically French holiday experience. Its own separate ski area compares favourably with many smaller regional resorts and being linked into the huge Grandes Rousses ski domain via Alpe d'Huez ensures that visitors of all standards of ability are sure to find something to like about this good all-rounder.

FURTHER INFORMATION

Auris-en-Oisans tourist information office:

☏ +33 (0)4 76 80 13 52   **ⓦ** www.auris-en-oisans.fr

PIEGUT CHAIR LIFT

8 mins

- 170 m (558 ft) vertical rise
- 968 m (1059 yd) long
- 1200 passengers/hour

An older, slower chair lift serving the out-of-town beginners' zone and its accompanying home run green pistes, departing from the central lifts base. The journey up provides a good vantage point from which to enjoy the superb views over the valley towards Les Deux Alpes and La Meije. At the mid-point of the journey, the lift line becomes more horizontal, travelling over wide and open snowfields, giving a pre-arrival opportunity to get your bearings: the piste over to the right is the Corniche blue, descending from the summit of Les Sures, above right; the piste below the lift line is the principal Les Crocus green; tucked in amongst them is the separate beginners' zone, ahead right.

On arrival, the dismount area is flat and wide; turn either left or right to begin Les Crocus green piste, U-turning back down the line of the lift; or, turn right only to follow the gentle track for the few metres over to the beginners' zone.

CHAMOIS / MARMOTTE

These are the beginners' zone pistes, tucked away at the tranquil margins of the ski area at the top of the Piegut sub-sector. The short gentle slopes are genuinely green-graded and are served by two easy button lifts. This is the most southern point in the Grandes Rousses domain, normally sunny and sheltered and providing beginners with an almost ideal environment in which to enjoy the learning process. The only downside to this out-of-town location is that there are no facilities here. To return to Auris station, follow Les Crocus green-piste home run.

LES CROCUS

The local piste map shows two green pistes running parallel to the line of the Piegut chair lift, both are named Les Crocus and both are merely variations of the same route, with very similar mild blue-equivalent profiles. Both start from the top of the Piegut chair lift, to either side on arrival, then range over a wide snowfield down the line of the arriving lift in this peaceful and sheltered tract of woodland. Despite a scarcity of piste markers, there is no difficulty in following the route; you can also ride over almost all of the inter-piste terrain for steeper and deeper lines, with mid-slope copses of fir trees giving more competent novices a chance to progress to a bit more adventurous freestyle action. Although the snowfield is wide and open, it is sheltered by the surrounding trees and hills.

Keeping furthest left allows you to join the Corniche blue piste for a steeper home run. Both Les Crocus pistes veer to the right, flowing together around the higher ground ahead before the final descent towards Auris. Off to the right, disappearing into the tree-line, is a gentle pisted road providing an attractive flatter route back to resort through the forest. Approaching Auris, keep furthest right around the top of the children's Snow Gardens to access the edge of the Place des Écrins; otherwise, keep going straight down under the chair lift on the wide main route to finish at the lower base area.

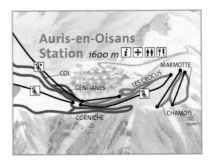

AURIS EXPRESS CHAIR LIFT

  6³/₄ mins ▲▼

- 267 m (876 ft) vertical rise
- 1787 m (1955 yd) long
- 1900 passengers/hour

The principal link lift at Auris station, accessing this area's best cruising reds and heading towards the connection with Alpe d'Huez. Departing from the base area, it rises directly over the main home runs, passing over the line of the Signal de l'Homme chair lift before cresting the ridge to travel downwards over the watershed on to the far flanks of the mountain. From here you can now see straight over to Alpe d'Huez.

At the arrival area, the other chair lift arriving ahead right is the short Louvets lift, serving the Eterlous green run and providing uplift from the Boucle Rochette Nordic circuit on the plain below. From the Auris Express, turn left to begin the Col blue (signed as the 'Chemin du Col'); or, go straight ahead, under the line of the Louvets chair lift, for the shared start to the Demoiselles and Le Gua greens. Because of the limitations in representing three-dimensional topography on a two-dimensional plane, these onward routes can be ambiguous on the piste map (see opposite for clarification).

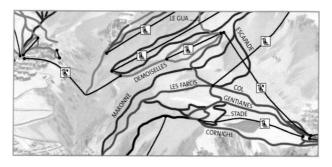

ONWARD LINKS

From the Auris Express chair lift:

Col blue – leaving to the left, initially as a road-like track (see page 202), back to Auris; also accessing the Maronne red and Les Farcis blue routes to Le Châtelard, plus the Signal de l'Homme chair lift to the eponymous summit.

Demoiselles green – poorly signed and slightly different than it appears on the local piste map: the route is a flat track leading directly away from the chair lift. It runs away at right angles from the Louvets lift-line, rather than parallel to it as suggested by the map. It eventually peels off down to the left, continuing across the flanks of the mountain to access the Alpauris chair lift (see over) linking with Alpe d'Huez; as well as reaching the Fontfroide lifts (see page 210) serving the principal Signal de l'Homme reds.

Le Gua green – the local piste map gives the illusion that this route is descending towards the top of the Auris Espress chair lift; the route is actually a flat traverse flowing away from the lift along with the Demoiselles green. After the Demoiselles leaves to the left, Le Gua continues straight on, gently traversing across the mountainside, slicing across all the pistes on the face of the Signal de l'Homme (stay alert when crossing – fast traffic from above right). It keeps going all the way over to a final steep section into the Gorge de Sarenne, merging with traffic coming from the Col de Cluy and the Glacier de Sarenne black runs, to run along the flat valley floor to the Chalvet, Lombards and Alpauris chair lifts (see pages 142, 212 and 200 respectively).

ALPAURIS CHAIR LIFT

6 mins ▲▼

- 299/195 m (981/640 ft) vertical rise/drop
- 1437 m (1572 yd) long
- 3000 passengers/hour

Interesting journey, interesting lift mechanism! This fast two-way chair lift links the Auris ski area directly with the Bergers base area at Alpe d'Huez, and vice versa, separated from one another by the deep Gorge de Sarenne. Rather than span the gorge, the lift line hugs the spectacularly steep sidewalls to descend to the floor of the ravine before climbing up the other side. When travelling from Auris, a clever piece of engineering declutches the lift at its valley-floor mid-point, allowing passengers to join there from the end of the long green-graded Le Gua track. Travelling from Alpe d'Huez, the chairs do not declutch and instead continue straight through this point to immediately climb up the steep wooded gorge wall towards Auris. Access to the lift therefore depends on which direction you are travelling in.

From Auris – the lift station is easily reached at the bottom of the Demoiselles green and Fontfroide red pistes. After descending into the gorge, the lift declutches and travels slowly through the mid-station, adding approximately one minute to the journey time. This is a get-on only point, so remain seated with the safety bar down; the lift then reconnects with the faster haul cable to climb up towards Alpe d'Huez. Approaching town, you travel through a tunnel under the end of the Altiport airstrip before arriving next to the Bergers commercial centre; dismount straight ahead for all onward links from this busy base area (see page 102). Last return lift to Auris is 16.30 hours.

From valley floor mid-station – towards Alpe d'Huez only. The control gates are automatic, but make sure that the chair

◔ *Alpe d'Huez viewed across the Gorge de Sarenne from Auris*

you are going for is actually unoccupied and that the safety bar
is raised. The journey takes 4½ minutes. The last lift up from this
station is at 17.00 hours.

From Alpe d'Huez – the lift station is situated on the far side
of the Bergers commercial centre, furthest away from the main
resort. The journey begins horizontally and dips down through
a short tunnel under the end of the Altiport airstrip, before
dropping steeply down into the gorge. There is no interruption in
the journey through the valley-floor mid-point, even though the
chairs travelling in the opposite direction declutch at a mid-
station to allow passengers to join there. On arrival at Auris,
U-turn to the right and ski down under the lift line to reach the
nearby Fontfroide lifts (see page 210) for all onward links.
L'Hermine bar/restaurant (see page 232) is at the far side of the
Fontfroide lifts base, a short stroll from the Alpauris arrival point.
The last return lift towards Alpe d'Huez is at 16.30 hours.

COL

Not that exciting for much of its length, but this run is a good first adventure for progressing beginners. It begins way-marked as the Chemin du Col, from the top of the Auris Express chair lift, joined from above left by a variation of the Fontfroide red. Both routes converge and narrow into a flat track, traversing across the open hillside. The steeper and deeper open slopes down to the right are more inviting for intermediates: the Maronne red accepts the invitation and drops off for a short but fast workout to join Les Farcis blue below, towards the Maronne chair lift at Le Châtelard (see page 207). The steep and mogulled swath of piste cutting straight down the opposite hillside is La Fuma black, with the Maronne chair lift rising up above it – even though this is at odds with the local piste map schematic and you would expect that side of the hill to be hidden from view.

The Col continues as a gentle track, following the contour-line towards a wide confluence area on the col De Maronne which marks the watershed with Auris. On reaching the line of the Signal de l'Homme chairlift, the route is joined from above left by the Escapade red: turn down to the right for the chair lift or to start Les Farcis blue; or, keep traversing straight ahead on the Col, which widens into a proper piste and develops a very respectable mild red profile for the home run to Auris, visible ahead below. Since the home run is a very tough blue, an easier escape route is the Nordic ski track – this peels off to the left and follows a pisted road all the way to the base station. Both home-run options finish beside the shared Auris Express and Sures chair lifts base.

▶ *Towards Les Sures from the Chemin de Col*

SURES CHAIR LIFT

4

5³/₄ mins

- 274 m (899 ft) vertical rise
- 751 m (822 yd) long
- 2400 passengers/hour

This lift's get-on point is shared with that for the Auris Express, at the main base area at Auris. Once inside the shared queuing-area corral, keep ahead left for the Sures lift; there is a tool point over to the right, nearer to the get-on point for the Auris Express. The lift climbs steeply up the face of Les Sures mountain, giving good views up the Col and Gentianes home-run blues and towards the summit of the Signal de l'Homme to the right, and over the Stade red and the steep and deep freeride slopes of Les Sures to the left.

Dismount is easy on arrival, straight on to the wide summit; with a couple of bench seats here making clipping into bindings easier for snowboarders; a piste patrol/first-aid hut is located ahead right. Turn right to begin the Gentianes blue and the Rhodos red, the latter accessing La Fuma black towards Le Châtelard; or, turn left for the Corniche blue, Stade red and the Snow Park. The Stade red is the station's competition course and is generally closed to the public; if it is open during your visit then it is a pleasant short blast straight back down to the base station.

CORNICHE

Beginning as a gentle glide along the summit of Les Sures, at the top of the Sures chair lift, this good blue then offers a couple of mild red pitches on its wide upper section before it sweeps down to flow gently across the open snowfields in the Piegut area, allowing you to vary the route there by joining the twin Les Crocus green routes (see page 197). Sticking to the left, the Corniche bends into the tree-line and develops a much better gradient again as it narrows through a mild chute, emerging just above the upper level of Auris resort and accompanying Les Crocus for the home run.

SNOW PARK

Auris's Snow Park is a small freestyle zone on the upper slopes of Les Sures, accessed from the start of the Corniche blue piste at the top of the Sures chair lift. The slope angle is good, but the range of modules is limited to a few kickers; the south-easterly orientation of this hillside means that snow conditions are not guaranteed. The park's best feature is that it is very accessible, with an easy circuit back to the lifts base and resort again after each run. On a sunny day with plenty of snow it will certainly provide freestyle improvers with a bit of fun.

GENTIANES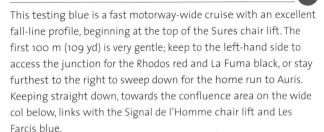

This testing blue is a fast motorway-wide cruise with an excellent fall-line profile, beginning at the top of the Sures chair lift. The first 100 m (109 yd) is very gentle; keep to the left-hand side to access the junction for the Rhodos red and La Fuma black, or stay furthest to the right to sweep down for the home run to Auris. Keeping straight down, towards the confluence area on the wide col below, links with the Signal de l'Homme chair lift and Les Farcis blue.

Sweeping in the direction of Auris, the Gentianes develops a testing red-equivalent slope angle and is often littered with small moguls. Nervous novices can avoid these by simply taking the easiest line out on to the wide col, then turn right to merge with the gentler parallel-running Col blue (see page 202). The run finishes as a fast schuss, making good links with all major lifts at the base station (check your speed approaching the base area).

RHODOS

A short, quiet red, perfect for a fast blast. Accessed from the summit of Les Sures via the upper section of the Gentianes blue – the junction departs to the left after just 100 m (109 yd). The start is a gentle glide until the slope flows off the summit area; the views from up here are superb, looking straight across the Gorges de Sarenne toward Alpe d'Huez. The piste then picks up a fast pace (stick to the left for the steepest lines) on a wide and open hillside, with a mid-section launch-point off some high ground. The Maronne chair lift arrives below left; keep above it and exit to the left to start La Fuma black, or continue descending ahead right to join Les Farcis blue towards Le Châtelard.

LA FUMA

Although short, this is a little gem. To find it, take the Rhodos red run, accessed via the upper Gentianes blue from the top of the Sures chair lift; the left-hand side of the Rhodos piste gives the steepest descent and veers over to the junction for La Fuma below, next to the arrival point for the Maronne chair lift. This mid-section of the route is simply a gentle glide under the line of the chair lift to reach the point where the descent truly begins. The real fun starts when the slope drops away steeply on the wooded hillside, frequently with a severely mogulled surface fitting a good black profile. The central to left-hand side offers the biggest challenge, although the

🔺 *Steep and gnarly, La Fuma black*

right-hand side is usually still a good test. Unfortunately the fun only lasts for around 350 m (383 yd) before ending abruptly by dropping out on to a flat variation route of Les Farcis blue. Control your finish and turn sharply left to join this for the next gentle section, giving you a change to catch your breath. After an easy blue-equivalent traverse through the woods, the route then swings down to the right on a wide and enjoyable mild red-profile stretch before meeting the main Les Farcis blue. Turn left to join this for the final cruise to Le Châtelard and the Maronne chair lift.

LES FARCIS

An enjoyable blue, providing competent novices with a manageable route towards Le Châtelard. It can be reached via the Col and Gentianes blues and the Rhodos red – the Col is the gentlest. Beginning at the same level as the get-on point for the Signal de l'Homme chair lift, the route dips gently over the col, heads away from Auris and runs around the flanks of the wooded hillside to the left. The Maronne red joins from above left at the mid-point and there is a variation route off into the trees to the left to meet the lower mild-red section of La Fuma black. The final approach to Le Châtelard is a lovely cruise and links well with the Maronne chair lift.

LE CHÂTELARD

A peaceful little rural outpost in the sheltered surroundings of the Maronne forest. It's a lovely spot at the extremities of the ski area and an authentic glimpse into the rural soul of the Oisans region. The hamlet is a 100 m (109 yd) flat stroll/skate away from the end of Les Farcis blue run and houses a pleasant small restaurant called La Forêt de Maronne (see page 231). Enterprising locals often set out a couple of tables and chairs at the base of the piste, serving hot drinks and snacks. The surrounding Alpine meadows are a good location for a picnic too.

🔺 *Approaching Le Châtelard on Les Farcis blue piste*

MARONNE CHAIR LIFT

7 mins

- 337 m (1106 ft) vertical rise
- 953 m (1043 yd) long
- 900 passengers/hour

The sole lift returning from Le Châtelard towards the core Auris ski area; easily reached at the end of Les Farcis blue piste. The journey up is a peaceful interlude in an active day, travelling above the treetops of the surrounding forest (the Forêt de Maronne), with views towards Huez village to the far left and passing over La Fuma black piste nearing the top. On arrival, go straight ahead on the easy off-ramp for all onward routes. The local piste map is confusing at this point as it doesn't show a connection with any piste returning to Auris, but the route does exist: straight ahead veering to the right around the contour-line, following the on-site directional signage for Auris to reach the Gentianes blue (this direction also links with the Signal de l'Homme chair lift). Otherwise, U-turn to the right on arrival, around the lift operator's hut, to start La Fuma black; or, go straight ahead veering down to the left to join the lower section of the Rhodos red towards Les Farcis blue.

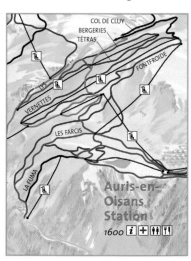

SIGNAL DE L'HOMME CHAIR LIFT

8 mins

- 443 m (1453 ft) vertical rise
- 1198 m (1311 yd) long
- 900 passengers/hour

Departing from the Col de Maronne above Auris, at the bottom of the Escapade red and accessible also via the Col and Gentianes blues. The journey up passes under the line of the Auris Express chair lift then up the steep flanks of the Signal to arrive near the summit. On arrival, dismount straight ahead to join the Fontfroide red, which is flowing past this point from above right; turn down left with it for all onward routes. A piste patrol/first-aid hut is above right on arrival.

FONTFROIDE

Starting at the summit of the Signal de l'Homme, at 2176 m (7137 ft), this excellent true red descends directly down the fall line, parallel to left of the Fontfroide chair lift. Shortly after the start, a variation route traverses off to the left towards the Escapade and Maronne reds in the direction of Auris and Le Châtelard. The prime Fontfroide piste continues straight down with a good variation in pitch; with some bumps, some steeper sections and some natural kickers. Almost the entire route can be seen stretching straight down below, with great views ahead towards Alpe d'Huez and the Pic Blanc massif. Halfway down, the piste is crossed by the route of Le Gua green, travelling from left to right – stay alert for crossing traffic. Nearing the bottom, check your speed before reaching the lifts: the Alpauris chair lift (see page 198) is on the immediate left, linking with Alpe d'Huez; otherwise, veer right for the Fontfroide lifts and l'Hermine bar/restaurant.

FONTFROIDE CHAIR LIFT

10 mins

- 452 m (1483 ft) vertical rise
- 1319 m (1443 yd) long
- 2200 passengers/hour

One of three lifts of the same name serving the steep face of the Signal de l'Homme. The two parallel-running button lifts on the left make exactly the same connections but take only six minutes to the top. The journey up rises parallel to the main pistes, giving a good chance to plan your descent on these excellent reds. On arrival, dismount straight ahead on to the flat summit: there are bench seats here for snowboarders to clip into their bindings, plus a piste patrol/first-aid hut to the right. Turn right for the Fontfroide red and to access the Maronne and Escapade reds towards Auris and Le Châtelard; turn left for the Bernettes, Tétras and Bergeries reds and the Cold de Cluy black.

VERNETTES

Wilder twin of the Fontfroide red, with even more lumps and bumps and opportunities to ride off into lightly wooded freeride terrain to the right of the piste, full of little gullies and natural kickers. The signed entrance at the top of the Signal de l'Homme requires you to skate up over an inclined mound; it is better therefore to ride down off the summit a little way on the Bergeries piste until you can leave to the left and pick up a better gradient to traverse to the Vernettes.

Stay alert when crossing Le Gua track mid-way down; nearing the bottom, check your speed and keep left for the Fontfroide lifts – the button lifts are nearest and easiest to reach. L'Hermine bar/restaurant is right at the finish area.

TÉTRAS

The Signal's least tame piste, far out to the left when looking up the mountain. If coming from the Fontfroide lifts, first take the wide top section of the shared Bergeries/Col de Cluy piste to reach the Lombards chair-lift arrival point. The Tétras then begins in earnest by dropping on to the face of the mountain, down the left-hand side of the Lombards lift line; the Vernettes red is parallel to the left and is reachable if you traverse across high enough. The Tétras takes a fairly direct fall-line route over the rough terrain on this side of the face, with plenty of opportunity to skip off into the woods and play on the gnarly ground to the sides amongst the well-spaced trees. Eventually you meet Le Gua green at the point where the Lys blue begins; you can cross Le Gua and continue straight down on the fall-line to finish on a lower section of the Lys blue below.

BERGERIES

The Bergeries officially begins immediately to the left on arrival from the Lombards chair lift, but the pisted route also starts from the top of the Fontfroide lifts, flowing off the wide and almost totally pisted summit down to the point where the Lombards lift arrives. The next section is then really just a continuation of the shared motorway-wide piste off the summit; keep to the right to access the entrance track for the Col de Cluy black, which goes straight on at the fence ahead; the Bergeries sweeps to the left. The piste then develops into a good fast cruise and continues as a wide standard red down to finish where it meets Le Gua green and Lys blue. Take either of these to reach the nearest lifts (only Le Gua links with the Chalvet lift).

LYS

Really just a link route and final section of the Bergeries red. Beginning at a junction on the long Le Gua green traverse, at the point where the Tétras red crosses. Just after the uppermost straight there is a tight hairpin turn to the left, the Bergeries red drops in from above right on this corner and the combined onward route is then a cruise across the hillside towards the line of the Lombards chair lift, where the piste turns sharply down to the right for a steeper good link to this lift below. Check your speed at the bottom as traffic is entering this area on the track (Le Gua green) emerging from the trees on the right. You can also link towards Alpe d'Huez from this level, by following the onward route of Le Gua green to the valley-floor mid-station of the Alpauris chair lift, but this is a real slog.

LOMBARDS CHAIR LIFT

- 565m (1854 ft) vertical rise
- 1515 m (1657 yd) long
- 1550 passengers/hour

This lift may be slow but it covers a lot of ground and rises to just below the summit of the Signal de l'Homme. As well as being directly accessible from the Auris sector's runs, it also provides a handy link into that sector for traffic coming from the Pic Blanc Sarenne run. The journey up is a good opportunity to check out the routes of the tough reds on the face of the Signal; on arrival, it's best to turn left for all routes (Tétras and Bergeries reds and Col de Cluy black) as the ground to the right is inclined; for the Tétras, U-turn left and go under the lift line to traverse across the top of the slopes until you can best drop on to the fall line.

COL DE CLUY ⬤

Not really a true black, but an enjoyable blast once it gets going. Starting at the top of the Signal de l'Homme, follow the wide pisted ridge shared with the uppermost part of the Bergeries red; the entrance to the Col de Cluy is at the fence ahead right, at the point where the Bergeries swings away to the left. The next part is no fun since it's just a flat access track, but the views certainly compensate: the impressive triple-peaked Aiguilles d'Arves are in the distance ahead and the awe-inspiring barbed peak of La Meije and the glacial summits above Les Deux Alpes are on the opposite side of the valley to the right.

Once past the flat access track, the piste spills off the entire shoulder of the mountain with a tough red-equivalent pitch, frequently mogulled and offering a myriad of possible lines of descent. Veering down to the left, the gradient eventually mellows to flow out on to the valley floor, although you can prolong the ride by dropping into the wide gully on the left.

The route merging from ahead right is the end of the epic Sarenne run from Pic Blanc; the piste joining from nearest left is Le Gua green; all routes converge and continue together along the valley-floor track towards the Chalvet and Lombards chair lifts.

🔺 *Towards Les Deux Alpes from the Col de Cluy*

POINT-TO-POINT ROUTES: COMPETENT NOVICES

ALPE D'HUEZ (ROND POINT DES PISTES) » VILLARD-RECULAS 1480

VILLARD-RECULAS 1480 » ALPE D'HUEZ (ROND POINT DES PISTES)

ALPE D'HUEZ (ROND POINT DES PISTES) » OZ-EN-OISANS STATION 1350

OZ-EN-OISANS STATION 1350 » ALPE D'HUEZ (ROND POINT DES PISTES)

ALPE D'HUEZ (ROND POINT DES PISTES) » VAUJANY 1250

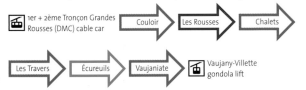

VAUJANY 1250 » ALPE D'HUEZ (ROND POINT DES PISTES)

Vaujany-Alpette cable car Alpette-Rousses cable car Le Belvédère Couloir

1er Tronçon

ALPE D'HUEZ (BERGERS) » AURIS-EN-OISANS STATION 1600

Alpauris chair lift Fontfroide chair lift Fontfroide Col

AURIS-EN-OISANS STATION 1600 » ALPE D'HUEZ (BERGERS)

Auris Express chair lift Demoiselles Alpauris chair lift

ALPE D'HUEZ (ROND POINT DES PISTES) » MONTFRAIS 1650

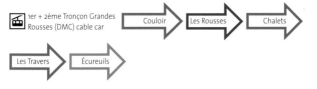

1er + 2ème Tronçon Grandes Rousses (DMC) cable car Couloir Les Rousses Chalets

Les Travers Écureuils

MONTFRAIS 1650 » ALPE D'HUEZ (ROND POINT DES PISTES)

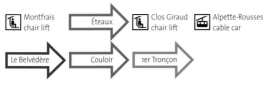

Montfrais chair lift Éteaux Clos Giraud chair lift Alpette-Rousses cable car

Le Belvédère Couloir 1er Tronçon

ALPE D'HUEZ (ROND POINT DES PISTES) » HUEZ

HUEZ » ALPE D'HUEZ (ROND POINT DES PISTES)

Télèvillage gondola lift   Télècentre bucket lift

HUEZ » ALPE D'HUEZ (BERGERS)

Télèvillage gondola lift   Eclose chair lift   Bergers chair lift

ALPE D'HUEZ (BERGERS) » 2100 AREA INTERCHANGE

Marmottes I gondola lift

2100 AREA INTERCHANGE » ALPE D'HUEZ (BERGERS)

2700 AREA INTERCHANGE » ALPE D'HUEZ (BERGERS)

POINT-TO-POINT ROUTES: GOOD INTERMEDIATES AND ABOVE

ALPE D'HUEZ (ROND POINT DES PISTES) » VILLARD-RECULAS 1480

Signal chair lift → Les Vallons → La Forêt → Villard

VILLARD-RECULAS 1480 » ALPE D'HUEZ (ROND POINT DES PISTES)

TSD Le Villarais chair lift → Signal

ALPE D'HUEZ (ROND POINT DES PISTES) » OZ-EN-OISANS STATION 1350

1er Tronçon Grandes Rousses (DMC) cable car → Poutran → L'Olmet → Champclotury

OZ-EN-OISANS STATION 1350 » ALPE D'HUEZ (ROND POINT DES PISTES)

Poutran I + II gondola lifts → 1er Tronçon

ALPE D'HUEZ (ROND POINT DES PISTES) » VAUJANY 1250

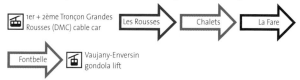

1er + 2ème Tronçon Grandes Rousses (DMC) cable car → Les Rousses → Chalets → La Fare → Fontbelle → Vaujany-Enversin gondola lift

VAUJANY 1250 » ALPE D'HUEZ (ROND POINT DES PISTES)

ALPE D'HUEZ (BERGERS) » AURIS-EN-OISANS STATION

AURIS-EN-OISANS STATION 1600 » ALPE D'HUEZ (BERGERS)

MONTFRAIS 1650 » ALPE D'HUEZ (ROND POINT DES PISTES)

ALPE D'HUEZ (ROND POINT DES PISTES) » HUEZ

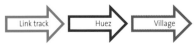

HUEZ » ALPE D'HUEZ (ROND POINT DES PISTES)

Télèvillage gondola lift   Télècentre bucket lift

HUEZ » ALPE D'HUEZ (BERGERS)

Télèvillage gondola lift   Eclose chair lift   Bergers chair lift

---

ALPE D'HUEZ (BERGERS) » 2100 AREA INTERCHANGE

Marmottes I gondola lift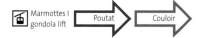

ALPE D'HUEZ (BERGERS) » 2700 AREA INTERCHANGE

Marmottes I gondola lift  2ème Tronçon Grandes Rousses (DMC) cable car

---

2700 AREA INTERCHANGE » ALPE D'HUEZ (BERGERS)

MOUNTAIN BARS & RESTAURANTS

The Grandes Rousses domain has a wealth of on-piste bars and restaurants, well spaced out so that you're never more than a couple of runs or a lift away from a refuelling and refreshment point. The largest are busy canteens, but there is also an excellent selection of cosier, more authentic Oisans mountain restaurants, where the fare on offer is centred on classic regional dishes, the ambiance is warmer and the service more personal.

All venues provide a full catering service from around 11.30–15.00 hours. They also provide a full bar and snacks' service all day, and almost all of them have WCs, mostly serviced and levying a small charge. Many of the venues can also be reached by non-skiers, either via the well-prepared walking/snowshoeing trails or by taking one of the many ski lifts which are accessible to pedestrians with a special Pedestrians' Pass (see page 82).

ALPE D'HUEZ BASE

Because the resort of Alpe d'Huez is so extensive, the number and variety of bars and restaurants close to, and easily accessible from, the base slopes is immense. The easiest areas to reach on-piste are the Rond Point des Pistes area and the commercial centre at Bergers. It's also possible to use specially provided link tracks, along the bottom of the Signal slopes immediately above town, to access the pisted Tunnel de Grandes Rousses under the route du Signal road and continue gliding into the heart of the Vieil Alpe quarter to reach the venues based in and around the old village centre. Most of the town restaurants only serve lunch from 12.00–14.00 hours.

◐ *Combe Haute auberge restaurant, Gorge de Sarenne*

TOWN SECTOR

The bustling 2100 and 2300 area interchanges, overlooking the wide and open slopes above Alpe d'Huez, house two of the largest venues in the domain. They are big and brash, but they offer a non-stop all-day food service and are very easy to get to and ride away from. Additionally, there are four good mountain chalet venues dotted around this home sector, offering a more refined experience in less hectic surroundings.

Chantebise 2100 €€ A huge establishment with massive terraces at the 2100 area interchange, right next to the Grandes Rousses (DMC) cable car mid-station. The terraces are on two levels – the uppermost is the restaurant terrace, with table service for all food and drinks, while the lower terrace has masses of deckchairs and also has table service, but for snacks and drinks only. There is also a quick snack kiosk at the entrance on to the terraces nearest the lift station entrance.

Some gear racks are provided, but nowhere near enough for a venue of this size and the entrance area quickly gets littered with skis and snowboards strewn on the ground. A good tip is to use the quieter steps at the far end of the terraces, nearest the lake plateau, as there is a lot more room to leave gear here.

The interior bar and dining room are bright, but quite plain. One great feature is the big conservatory-style extension, which can slide open completely, effectively bringing the interior dining saloon outside on the sunniest days.

Food on offer is brasserie standard, with a strong emphasis on pizzas and salads, but there is a fair range of regional classics such as gratin and tartiflette too. ☏ +33 (0)4 76 80 40 21

Chalet du Lac Besson €€ A lovely venue tucked away at the far side of the frozen lake plateau stretching away behind the main 2100 area buildings. The restaurant specifically serves the Boucle des Lacs Nordic circuit and the accompanying pedestrian route, corresponding to the Boulevard des Lacs blue piste on the standard piste map. The approach to the venue is by nature very flat, but it's definitely worth the effort. The wooden chalet has an attractive interior with an open fireplace. There is a fair-sized terrace overlooking the plateau towards the 2100 area and a good number of deckchairs set out on the snow at what is the edge of the lake in summer.

The extensive menu includes a good range of meats grilled on the wood fire, plus raclette, ravioles, crozets and other Savoie and Isère specialities. Snacks are also available from a grill service on the terrace. ☎ +33 (0)4 76 80 65 37

La Plage des Neiges €+ The closest on-mountain bar/restaurant to the main Snow Park, located at the top of the Babars I button lift. The venue is also accessible from the Sagnes green piste, the Boucle de Poutran Nordic circuit and pedestrian route. There are steps up from the button lift arrival area, but these can be tricky when icy; it is best to stroll around to the front of the building and enter via the terrace. The venue is a large wooden chalet with a terrace overlooking the Snow Park and central beginners' slopes; the pleasant interior has large picture windows with good views and plenty of natural daylight.

The range of food on offer is based around standard international fare such as omelettes, pasta, burgers and pizzas, but also with tartiflette, mixed grill dishes and a range of salads.
☎ +33 (0)4 76 80 39 56

Marmottes €€ A huge cafeteria at the 2300 area interchange with lots of deckchairs on the plateau beside the lifts' structure. A snack kiosk serves this area and there is also waiter service for snacks/drinks. Inside, there are a couple of Internet stations, a large bar and a big self-service restaurant. The range of food is cafeteria-style: a basic salad buffet and a choice of around six hot dishes (spaghetti bolognese, goulash, chicken and chips, etc).

Doors lead out to the massive terrace – a platform cantilevered out over the hillside, affording sweeping vistas over the Town sector slopes and resort below, and over the Signal de l'Homme slopes at Auris to Les Deux Alpes in the distance beyond; there is a waiter service for snacks/drinks. The venue also houses a separate à la carte restaurant called La Grange, which has its own enclosed patio off the main terrace and a segregated section in the main interior. This section's food selection is a bit more refined and includes grills, tartiflette and fondues, a fair salad buffet and a range of good value set menus. ❶ +33 (0)4 76 80 32 36

● *Overlooking Alpe d'Huez from La Cabane de Poutat*

La Cabane de Poutat €€+ A popular, good quality venue above Bergers, which is accessible via the Vachettes blue piste and on foot via the pedestrians trail under the Marmottes I gondola lift line. This is an attractive wooden chalet with a good-sized terrace and plenty of deckchairs, overlooking the entire lower ski area and resort. There is a snack bar kiosk on the terrace, plus waiter service.

The interior bar and dining room are homely, with quality furnishings and an open fireplace. Hangers are provided for jackets, and there are slippers to change into for a break from your boots. Food standard and presentation is high, with tartiflette, raclette and pot au feu on the menu. 'Luxury' gourmand specials are also offered, plus a good range of desserts and a decent wine list. ☎ +33 (0)4 76 80 42 88

L'Altibar €€+ A pleasant chalet restaurant located at the Altiport, with a dining room and terrace overlooking the airstrip, reached via a pisted link track through the Altiport chalets suburb. This is a slightly unusual choice, away from the core ski area yet easily reachable from the pistes, with the added interest of being able to watch the take offs and landings of the light aircraft and helicopters on the pisted runway. There is an excellent selection of refined quality meals and a fair number of fish dishes.
☎ +33 (0)4 76 80 41 15

MID SECTOR

There are no mountain bars or restaurants in this sector, however, since all of the lower Town sector slopes are immediately accessible as a continuation of all Mid sector routes, the lack of on-piste venues on these upper slopes isn't really an issue.

PIC BLANC / GLACIER SECTOR

Again, there are no bars or restaurants in the uppermost reaches of this sector but, as with the Mid sector, it's very easy simply to descend on-piste to the Town sector venues. The one good venue that is directly accessible is reached when completing the circuit from the epic Sarenne run, down in the Gorge de Sarenne.

Combe Haute €€ An attractive establishment set in a lovely setting, deep in the Gorge de Sarenne at the base of the Chalvet chair lift, reached at the finish of the Sarenne black run (also from the Col de Cluy black and Le Gua green pistes from the Auris sector and La Mine red piste from the Alpe d'Huez side). Its sheltered, wooded location beside the gentle stream of the Sarennes river, is at the base of the severe rock face which looms directly above this part of the ravine, making this a very impressive site (see picture on page 220).

The venue is a big wooden chalet (which also operates as an Auberge for overnight stays) with a fair-sized, piste-side snack bar terrace and a separate small restaurant with an exterior balcony dining area and a cosy interior saloon. Good wholesome fare is served in the restaurant, including spaghetti bolognese, chilli con carne, mountain charcuterie, salads and grilled meats. The snack bar area offers hot dogs, chips, burgers, soup, etc, but is let down by only providing plastic cutlery and serving food in plastic takeaway containers. Nevertheless, this is a welcome pit stop after the marathon descent from the summit of Pic Blanc. Don't linger too late in the afternoon, though, or you will miss the last lifts out of the gorge! This venue can also be reached via the Boucle d'Huez Nordic/snowshoeing route. ☎ +33 (0)4 76 80 61 38

SIGNAL / VILLARD SECTOR

There are just two on-mountain venues here, but both are good. The Signal slopes are immediately above Alpe d'Huez town, so there is plenty of off-mountain choice near at hand too.

Le Signal €€ Situated almost on the summit of the Signal de la Grande Sure, directly above Alpe d'Huez and with an exceptional panorama over the resort and surrounding ski area. There is a terrace with BBQ and the interior bar/restaurant has large picture windows with the same views. The decor here is very traditional with an old wood-burning stove, green and red paintwork and soft furnishings, with pine cones and candles lending the venue a festive feel. The menu is focused on wholesome regional mountain fare, including tartiflette, fondue and raclette, grills and pizzas cooked in a wood-fired oven, plus a wide range of home-made pastries. Open on night-skiing evenings; accessible by pedestrians using the Grande Sure chair lift. ☏ +33 (0)4 76 80 39 54

La Bergerie €€ This is the sole on-mountain catering on the Villard-Reculas slopes, located just above the base area in the middle of the home run pistes and accessible from the lower base area using either the Tortue or Langaret button lifts. It is a beautifully rustic old mountain refuge, constructed with sun-aged timbers and with a terrace overlooking the base slopes towards the peaks of the Chaîne de Belledonne. Unusual, piste-side bar stools encircle the terrace; the interior is decorated with old Alpine farming equipment and pioneering skiing memorabilia. A wide range of salads and grills, home-made pastries and a good range of speciality beers on draught is available. ☏ +33 (0)4 76 80 36 83

VAUJANY / OZ SECTOR

Although ranging away from the core ski area, this quieter sector boasts a number of good on-piste venues. Most are small privately-owned traditional mountain cabins, fitting many people's ideal of what authentically typical mountain restaurants should be like. They are all easy to find, clustered at key crossing points at the sides of the main pistes, all at easily accessible mid-altitude locations.

Perce-Neige €€ This rustic mountain refuge is one of the area's best original mountain restaurants. It is perched in a commanding position overlooking the valley towards the peaks of the Chaîne de Belledonne, at the base of the Champ Clotury button lift, and accessible via the Poutran red piste, Boulevard des Lutins blue piste and Lutins green piste, on the descent towards Oz-en-Oisans. The venue has a fair-sized terrace and cosy, homely interior dining room with an open fireplace, which is decorated with lots of old farming implements and old-fashioned ski gear.

A good range of wholesome regional mountain fare is on offer, mostly centred on roast meat dishes; fondue, salads, pasta, home-made tarts and desserts are also available. Cooked breakfasts 09.00–11.00 hours. ☎ +33 (0)4 76 80 69 67

Le Croc' Neige €€ This is a tiny, simple snack bar/restaurant at the quiet mid-point of L'Olmet red run on the way down to Oz-en-Oisans. The small terrace has superb views over the valley to the Chaîne de Belledonne. Piste-side deckchairs and a cosy interior with open fireplace. No fuss grills, baked potatoes, sandwiches, pasta and snacks available. ☎ +33 (0)4 76 80 33 04

Auberge de l'Alpette €+

A simple, welcoming, family-run mountain refuge and one of the oldest-established mountain restaurants in the area. Located on the Carrelet green piste, just below the plateau at l'Alpette, it is also accessible via the Bartavelles red piste. Although off the main interchange, this point is

▲ *Al fresco lunch at l'Alpette 2050*

very accessible. L'Alpette button lift is nearby, for returning up to l'Alpette 2050, and the Alpette red run towards Oz-en-Oisans is a little way ahead. The venue has a fair-sized terrace with a view overlooking the valley and peaks of the Chaîne de Belledonne, and the interior saloon, though plain and homespun, is nevertheless inviting and warm.

A fair range of good, wholesome regional specialities is served, along with lighter snacks and a wide range of crêpes and home-made desserts. ❶ +33 (0)4 76 80 70 00

La P'Oz Chez Passoud € An unpretentious, old-fashioned snack bar and restaurant on the edge of the plateau, with great views from the fair-sized terrace, with some deckchairs and a plain interior bar/dining saloon. If coming into this area via Les Rousses red run, this venue is the first on the left. Basic meals and snacks served, including pizzas, salads, chicken and chips, quiche and sandwiches. No table service. ❶ +33 (0)4 76 80 78 96

La Grange €+

This restaurant is an attractive small wooden cabin at the rear of the plateau at l'Alpette, immediately to the right if entering the area from Les Rousses red run. The terrace overlooks the plateau, in a sheltered position at the base of the cliffs of the Dôme des Petites Rousses, almost directly beneath the Alpette-Rousses cable car lift line. The atmosphere is animated, enlivened with rock and pop music. There is a small sledging piste to the front.

◖ *La Grange restaurant at l'Alpette 2050*

The speciality of the house is the range of wood-fired oven pizzas. Other choices include fillet steak and chips, grills and snacks such as paninis. ❶ +33 (0)4 76 11 03 66

Les Airelles €€ This lovely old rustic refuge is built into the bedrock at the side of the Écureuils green piste in the Montfrais satellite ski area. The two piste-side terraces have good views down the valley towards the peaks of the Chaîne de Belledonne. The cosy interior is like being in a cave, with different nooks and crannies in the warren-like structure.

An excellent range of traditional Oisans' specialities is available, together with an enticing selection of home-made tarts and desserts. ❶ +33 (0)4 76 80 79 78

Le Vaujaniat €€ A plain self-service, canteen-style restaurant located at the point where the Écureuils green and Étourneaux blue pistes converge, approaching the base area. A fair selection of simple salads, hot combination dishes and daily specials is served. ☎ +33 (0)4 76 80 71 87

Au P'Tit Truc This is a tiny, simple snack bar, no more than a little hut, at the Montfrais 1650 base area, just below the get-on point for the Vallonet chair lift and a short stroll from the Villette-Montfrais gondola lift upper station. Bar service and canned soft drinks available, plus a limited range of snacks.

AURIS SECTOR

Just a couple of on-piste venues at altitude here, but the small resort at the base station has a few snack bars and simple restaurants accessible from the lower slopes. The easiest to reach is just beside the Aurus Express and Sures chair lifts' get-on level.

La Forêt de Maronne €+ A small, family-run restaurant, not quite within the ski area but very easy to reach, just 100 m (109 yd) from the bottom of Les Farcis blue piste (also accessible via the Marrone red and La Fuma black pistes) at the hamlet of Le Châtelard. It is situated in a lovely location in a secluded Oisans' mountain hamlet at the outermost margins of the Grandes Rousses domain, surrounded by the peaceful Marrone forest and perfect for an unrushed, tranquil lunch away from the crowds.

The terrace is south-facing and the cosy interior is rustic. Serves regional mountain fare and grills, but also features some Spanish and Portuguese dishes. ☎ +33 (0)4 76 80 00 06

L'Hermine €+ This is a rustic mountain-chalet snack bar and restaurant situated on the Signal de l'Homme mountain at the bottom of the Vernettes and Fontfroide red pistes and the Demoiselles green piste, next to the Fontfroide lifts and just a short stroll from the Alpauris chair lift link with Alpe d'Huez. There is a fair-sized terrace, with bench-style tables/seating and some deckchairs, which faces up the Signal and looks up over the approaching pistes and the gnarly freeride terrain on the mountainside out beside the Tétras red run. There is a food and drink service counter on the terrace, but no table service. The interior has a very small, cosy dining room for rough weather days. A reasonable range of basic international dishes such as omelettes, salads, simple grills, lasagne and crepes is available. However, there aren't any WCs here. ☎ +33 (0)6 80 24 76 40

ALTERNATIVE ACTIVITIES

Alpe d'Huez is marketed as an all-round mountain-sports lifestyle resort, with something for everyone. To this end, the station also provides an excellent range of other activities to complement the principal downhill skiing. It's mostly focused on high-adrenaline sports, but with plenty of tamer fun activities to appeal to all ages and abilities too. Full details and bookings are available via the Central Tourist Office (La Maison de la Alpe) at place Joseph Paganon in the Vieil Alpe quarter of the resort. The local tourist offices in each of the satellite villages also coordinate the alternative activities in each of their respective stations; please see pages 155, 161, 185 or 195 for contact details.

ⓘ Activities may not be covered by travel insurance (see page 54).

LANGLAUF

Although Downhill skiing is Alpe d'Huez's prime focus, Nordic skiing, or 'langlauf', ('ski du fond' in French) is also taken very seriously by the station. Extensive, well-maintained cross-country circuits are located in six different settings, spread over four sectors (see over for details). Routes and access details are printed on a separate 'Plan Fondeur' piste map, which is available from the central tourist office, ski pass sales points and also at two dedicated Nordic-skiing information/ski pass sales cabins located at:
1) the start of the Boucle de Pierre Ronde circuit at Bergers.
2) at the far end of the free Grenouilles button lift heading away from the Rond Pont des Pistes area.

Both the ESF and ESI ski schools offer Nordic ski tuition. See page 73 for details of Nordic ski passes.

◀ *It's not all Downhill, Alpe d'Huez has extensive Nordic pistes too*

LANGLAUF CIRCUITS

Boucle de Pierre Ronde This trail begins at the Bergers area of Alpe d'Huez, just under the line of the Alpauris chair lift near the end of the Altiport runway. After passing through the Altiport area, this gentle circuit heads out towards the lip of the Gorge de Sarenne and the open snowfields under the line of the Chalvet chair lift. Blue piste 4 km (2½ miles) long.

Boucle d'Huez An open-ended trail departing from the side of the main road just below Huez village centre. This interesting journey takes you deep into the Gorge de Sarenne and along the valley floor to the Combe Haute auberge restaurant (see page 226). Blue piste 4 km (2½ miles) long.

Boucle de Poutran An extensive circuit which is one of the station's key Nordic courses, leading to the higher level Boucle des Lacs circuit. Leaving from the Rond Point des Piste base area, the piste follows the line of the free-of-charge Grenouilles button lift and snakes up through the margins of the Jeux beginners' zone to the plateau on the Col de Poutran, which marks the watershed into the Vallée de l'Eau d'Olle and affords fabulous views towards the Chaîne de Belledonne. The circuit area also houses a dedicated Nordic skiers hostal (called the 'Foyer de Fond') which has a dormitory for overnight stays. ☎ +33 (0)4 76 80 37 38. This circuit can also be joined at its highest level via the Poutran II gondola lift from Oz-en-Oisans. Blue piste 10 km (6¼ miles) long.

Boucle des Lacs The principal circuit at Alpe d'Huez, high and snow-sure on the frozen Besson lake plateau beyond the 2100 area interchange, accessed as a continuation of the Boucle de

Poutran circuit or from any of the major lifts which reach this level. As well as skirting around the frozen lake, this route also extends all the way to/from the interchange area on the plateau at l'Alpette 2050. Good varied terrain, great views and a respectable length. Red piste 20 km (12½ miles) long.

Boucle de la Rochette Located in the Auris sector and accessed directly by an on-piste route from the base station, or via the Auris Express chair lift. The route shares the hillside above Auris base area with the Alpine ski pistes, but then ranges out on its own to a wide plateau on the edge of the Gorge de Sarenne, giving sweeping vistas across the gorge to Alpe d'Huez and Huez village. The pisted route loops back towards Auris, or you can use the Louvets chair lift to reach the two-way Auris Express chair lift. Blue/Red piste 4 km (2½ miles) long.

Boucle de pré Reynaud A compact, wooded trail at the edge of Oz-en-Oisans station. Quite limited, but easily accessible from the village and providing Nordic novices and weekend dabblers with an attractive and easy circuit. Blue piste 4 km (2½ miles) long.

NON-SKIERS

All of the Nordic circuits have accompanying walkers snow-paths and many ski lifts are accessible to foot passengers, however you will need to purchase a Pedestrian Pass to use them (see page 82 for details). A ski pass is not always necessary to participate in the alternative activities on offer; please enquire at the time of booking.

SNOWSHOEING

Modern showshoes are made of lightweight materials and are very easy to master. They work by spreading your weight over a wider surface area, allowing you to walk more easily over deep snow, using a pair of ski poles for balance. Referred to locally as raquettes, they are a great way for all visitors to get out into the more tranquil corners of the mountains, where you're more likely to spot Alpine wildlife. Follow the way-marked walkers routes or hire a guide and head off into the wilds. Equipment hire is available at most good ski rental shops.

ICE SKATING

Alpe d'Huez has an Olympic-size, outdoor ice rink centrally located on the avenue des Jeux. This great facility is a real focal point in the resort, open to the sky and the views and with free spectator seating. Curling is also played, and the tourist office entertainment team organize regular free trial sessions. Entrance is free with a current VISALP skipass; skate hire is available on-site, although this is at a small extra charge. ⏱ Open daily 10.00–23.00 hours; floodlit at night.

Vaujany and Oz-en-Oisans also have rinks. Opening times and entrance conditions are similar to the main Alpe d'Huez facility, but are more reliant on seasonal demand.

ICE CLIMBING

This is an amazing adventure sport for real adrenaline junkies. A mountain guide teaches you the basics of climbing with ice axes and crampons and then you get to scale an incredible frozen waterfall. Bookings available through the Bureau des Guides (see page 77 for contact details).

SNOWMOBILES

This thrilling motorsport is consistently the most requested alternative wintersports activity. A dedicated circuit is marked out on the open plateau at the frozen Lac de Besson, stretching away from the 2100 area interchange. Each snowmobile can carry two people; drive yourself or hang on tight as a passenger. Charged per machine for a duration of 10, 20 or 30 minutes.

🔺 *Snowmobiling above Alpe d'Huez*

QUADS

Blast around Alpe d'Huez's pisted quad-bike circuit or tour the town accompanied by a guide. The circuit and tour departure point is at the circuit information cabin on the rue du 93 éme RAM. Charged per person for a duration of 6, 10 or 15 minutes for the circuit, or 20 or 45 minutes for the resort tour. 🕐 Circuit open daily 09.00–dusk 🌐 www.quadmania.fr.st

ICE DRIVING

The Circuit de l'Oisans ice-driving track, on the rue du 93 éme RAM in Alpe d'Huez, is a permanent course that hosts the international Andros Trophy race. It is open to the public for tyre testing and ice driving lessons and is a fantastic opportunity to thrash a car around a pisted circuit, whilst learning the basics of safe winter driving. 🕐 Open daily 09.00–12.00 and 17.00–20.00 hours.

FLYING

The Alps are even more breathtaking when seen from a bird's-eye viewpoint and Alpe d'Huez offers many ways to take to the air. The town's Altiport is named after Henri Giraud, a local enthusiast who pioneered Alpine flying and the techniques required to take off and land on snow. Its pisted runway is in almost constant use on fair weather days and it is an important transport hub for the resort. It is easily reached on-piste from above the Bergers base area or by ski bus from town. The L' Altiport bar/restaurant here (see page 225) is great for watching take-offs and landings.

Airplane Sightseeing flights These are available over the Grandes Rousses, the surrounding resorts and even over the summit of Mont Blanc, Western Europe's highest peak. Aeroclub de Dauphiné ☎ 33 (0)4 76 11 35 81. Ultra Light Motorized aircraft trips are also available www.alpedhuez-ulm.com

Helicopter Heli-skiing is banned in France, but you can arrange for connections to nearby Les Deux Alpes from the helipad at the Altiport. Sightseeing trips and transfers to/from airport are also possible. SAF Isère ☎ +33 (0)4 76 80 65 49

Hang glider / Paraglider Alternatively, launch off the summit of the Signal harnessed into a hang glider or steerable paragliding canopy, in tandem with a professional pilot, for an incredible sensation of soaring silently above the slopes, with skiers far below your feet, before landing on the slopes at the Rond Point des Pistes for a real 007 effect. Information and bookings kiosk on the pistes at the Rond Point des Pistes. Delta Evasion ☎ +33 (0)6 08 32 49 59 Ⓦ www.deltaevasion.com

GROTTE DE GLACE (ICE CAVE)

Every winter season, a mass of dense snow is specially created by the station's snowmaking plant to build this fascinating structure; a team of artists then burrow over 100 m (328 ft) into it to create a chamber of ephemeral artworks. Their sculptures follow a different theme every year and are backlit to glow eerily in the muted light. Situated behind the shared Pic Blanc/Grandes Rousses (DMC) cable car station at the 2700 area interchange. Accessible on-piste and by pedestrians; small entrance charge. ● Open daily 10.00–16.00 hours. ⓦ www.grottedeglace.com

SPORTS CENTRES & SWIMMING POOLS

The Palais des Sports et des Congrès Avenue de Brandes houses Alpe d'Huez's excellent municipal sports facilities: the complex offers a well-equipped gymnasium, step and aerobic classes, squash and indoor tennis courts, climbing wall, golf driving range, archery, basketball and an indoor swimming pool. Free admission with VISALP skipass (small charge requested at peak times for some activities; equipment hire extra). ● Open daily 10.00–20.45 hours.

The resort also has an outdoor heated swimming pool, just up from the ice rink on the avenue des Jeux, open daily 11.00–20.00 hours. Free admission with VISALP skipass.

Espace Loisirs de Vaujany Located in the valley just below Vaujany's central lifts station, accessible by a funicular elevator and then a short path from the rear of the lifts station, or simply from the road leading down to the centre's car park. The centre's facilities include an indoor swimming pool with flume slide, fitness suite, Turkish bath, sauna and Jacuzzi. Free admission with the VISALP ski pass.

APRÈS SKI

Once the sun has set, the focus for fun turns away from the pistes and towards the attractions of the resorts and the social side of the snowsports experience. Alpe d'Huez attracts a cosmopolitan, sophisticated clientele and has the facilities to match: those with an addiction to activity can continue to ski

◆ *Avenue des Jeux*

on some evenings during the week and should be more than satisfied with the extensive range of sports and leisure amenities available. For later in the evening, there is a wide range of bars and restaurants and the town has a reputation for lively nightlife. Evenings in the surrounding satellite resorts revolve around unhurried dinners and convivial conversation.

NIGHT SKIING & SLEDGING

From 17.30–19.30 hours on Tuesdays and Thursdays, the Signal stadium above Alpe d'Huez is floodlit for night skiing; access is free to all current VISALP skipass holders. The piste is 1250 m (1368 yd) long and has a vertical drop of 250 m (820 ft), so it's a serious enough run to be more than a gimmick.

Across town, on the same evenings and during the same hours, the sledging hill at l'Eclose is also floodlit and the Eclose chair lift that serves it is also free of charge for current VISALP ski pass holders (sledges are not provided).

PAMPERING

The trend for 'wellness' holidays in the Alpine resorts continues to grow and the available facilities are improving all the time. Many of the larger 3- and 4-star quality hotels have their own in-house hydrotherapy suites, usually attached to fitness rooms. Additionally, Alpe d'Huez has two beauty parlours to pamper and pummel:

Laurence Bondet, avenue des Jeux: sports and relaxing massages, facials, body moisturizing and toning treatments, manicures, pedicures and waxing. ☏ +33 (0)4 76 80 31 73

Parapharmacie des Bergers, centre commercial des Bergers: offers a range of beauty treatments, including facials, body moisturizing and toning, manicures, pedicures and waxing. ☏ +33 (0)4 76 11 39 25

RETAIL THERAPY

Alpe d'Huez is an extensive conurbation with a year-round population and therefore has a fair range of shops, although like all ski resorts most of these are mountain sports equipment and clothing stores. The main shopping areas are the avenue des Jeux and the Bergers commercial centre, with further small retail clusters on the route d'Huez and the route de la Poste (see town plans on pages 67 and 69). As well as the usual plethora of sports outlets, there are a fair number of boutiques, regional products delicatessens, patisseries and bakeries, souvenir shops, several well-stocked large supermarkets and also a couple of pharmacies/ perfumeries, specialist eyewear boutiques, photographic studios, newsagents and bookshops. There are also several banks, most with 24-hour cash machines, a post office and a number of launderettes.

CAFÉS & RESTAURANTS

Alpe d'Huez has plenty of snack bars and cafés and more than 50 restaurants; a lot of the restaurants are quite average, with most offering similar bland international fare heavily reliant on pizzas and snack-orientated menus. However, there are a good number of more committed and noteworthy serious restaurants too. Most are open at lunchtime and in the evenings from 19.00-23.00 hours. The following are a selection of some of the best (see town plans on pages 65 and 67). In the satellite villages things are on a much smaller scale, but there are one or two gems that stand out above the other standard pizza and pasta venues.

ALPE D'HUEZ

Au P'tit Creux €€+ Small, family-run venue in the Vieil Alpe quarter, on the piste-side footpath between the route du Siou-Coulet and the Maison de l'Alpe tourist office. Homely, unpretentious farmhouse-style decor but with an aspirational menu featuring seasonally influenced fish- and fine meat-based dishes. ☎ +33 (0)4 76 80 62 80

Au Grenier €€ Venue with an attractive, cosy interior with a barrel-shaped ceiling located on avenue de Brandes. Creative fish dishes and Savoyard classics. ☎ +33 (0)4 76 80 64 11

Le Génépi €€ Lovely, rustic old farmhouse on route Romaine in the heart of the old village in the Vieil Alpe quarter, with exposed beams and roughcast walls. With an open fire and cosy ambiance, this venue specializes in classic regional cuisine such as raclette, tartiflette and pierrades. ☎ +33 (0)4 76 80 36 22

La Fondue en Folie €€+ As the name suggests, fondues are the speciality here – and how! From cheese fondues through to many different meat fondues to dessert chocolate fondues, every variation you can think of and more. It's very popular, so booking is recommended. Located inside the Galerie de l'Ours Blanc on avenue des Jeux. ☎ +33 (0)6 74 09 68 44

La Cordée €+ A plain but pleasant venue with an unusual mix of cuisine on offer: specializing in Irish-themed dishes such as beef in Guinness and 'surf & turf' (beef with prawns). Also Thai curry and Savoyard specialities – around the world in 80 minutes! Vegetarian choices too. Regular live music.
Rue de la Meije. ☎ +33 (0)4 76 80 35 39

L' Authentique €€ Housed on the ground floor of a modern block but wood-clad and decorated to resemble a chalet. Specializing in Italian cuisine, with a large range of pastas, lasagne, osso bucco, etc. Top end of avenue des Jeux. ☎ +33 (0)4 76 80 43 31

Chilly Powder €€ Thai, Indian and Chinese food and Asian beers. Laid back atmosphere and popular with resort workers. Open at lunchtime and close to the Rond Point des Pistes. Top end of avenue du Rif Nel. ☎ +33(0)4 76 80 49 56

Les Primtemps de Juliette €+ Quaint, quality café and tea room in the attractive hotel of the same name, at the bottom of avenue des Jeux. Fairy lights frame the attractive exterior; the interior is spotless and bright and offers speciality coffees and ice cream. Occasional live accordion music.
☎ +33 (0)4 76 11 44 38

La Pomme de Pin €€ Quality restaurant with gourmet aspirations and which offers a salon de thé and cocktail bar service too. Savoyard and Oisans mountain specialities such as tartiflette, raclette, pierrade, fondues and ravioles. Welcoming staff and attentive service. Good value for a venue of this quality. Lower end of avenue des Jeux. ❶ +33 (0)4 76 80 42 34

Le Taburle €+ Hard to miss because of its sheer size and location, at the foot of the pistes in the heart of the Rond Point des Pistes area. There is a huge terrace served by a snack kiosk during the day, and the big interior restaurant specializes in wood-fire oven pizzas, pastas, salads and omelettes. A popular lunchtime venue; accessible from the top end of avenue du Rifnel. ❶ +33 (0)4 76 80 36 25

VAUJANY

La Remise €€ Quality establishment in the Galerie Marchande square in the upper level of the village. Attractive, rustically decorated interior and a lunchtime patio in the square. Wood-fire oven pizzas, fondues, raclette, tartiflette and mountain charcuterie, plus crêpes and waffles throughout the day. ❶ +33 (0)4 76 80 77 11

AURIS

L' Aurienchon €€ A simple but very welcoming small restaurant located down in the hamlet of Les Cours, immediately below the resort of Auris Station. Worth a taxi ride or a drive. Features ostrich and kangaroo fillets, plus live 'cabaret' music/singer. ❶ +33 (0)4 76 80 06 43

BARS & CLUBS

Alpe d'Huez is a big enough resort to offer lots of choice of bars, music bars and even some proper nightclubs, yet it still has plenty of quiet corners and mellower venues in which to pass the evenings too; with so much competition, most bars make a real effort to plan varied programmes of theme nights and events and there are live bands playing most evenings somewhere in town. The avenue des Jeux and the route du Coulet have the greatest concentration of bars and clubs and the most lively atmosphere. Most bars are open until around 01.00 hours, nightclubs until 03.00 hours. The following are some of the most popular (town plans on pages 65 and 67).

ALPE D'HUEZ

Freeride Music pub with a tiny dance floor and late night DJs or live music. Infamous for its fire-eating staff and the slide that leads down to the WCs – quicker than taking the stairs! Good extreme sports videos shown too. Avenue de Jeux.

O'Sharkeys Irish bar, featuring an airgun shooting gallery! Karaoke nights, live music, pool table and table football and big screen sports. Rue de la Grenouillère.

Le Sporting A massive venue on a raised level overlooking the ice rink on avenue des Jeux, housing an excellent typically Savoyard restaurant serving raclettes, tartiflettes, fondues and pierrades, and a lively piano bar with a nightly cabaret and dancing. Cocktails and table service and a good programme of entertainment. Suitable for an older, more sophisticated crowd.

Fun Café A big games arcade and bar underneath Le Sporting, beside the ice rink on avenue des Jeux. This is a roomy arcade with plenty of full-size arcade video games, plus pool tables, air hockey and table football.

Smithy's One of the resort's key pubs, with frequent live music and a legendary reputation for its tolerance of dancing on the tables. Good value 'fish bowl' cocktails, shots, pool table and table football. Route de Coulet.

Les Caves de l'Alpe Attractive chalet-style building on the route du Coulet, housing a decent Savoyard restaurant and with a discothèque in the basement. Slightly older crowd. International music policy with a Euro Dance bias.

Igloo / Tropicana Two nightclubs housed in the same building on route du Coulet. Both have decent music policies and frequent guest DJs and theme nights.

SPECIAL EVENTS

All of the Grandes Rousses stations have good and varied programmes of events and entertainments which are organized by dedicated resort animation teams; programme leaflets are printed on a weekly basis, distributed throughout the resorts and available from the local tourist offices.

For details of all major ski competitions and festivals, please go to our website **www.ski-ride.com**

OUT & ABOUT
Ideas for summer

OISANS AND BEYOND

Although this book is a specialist guide to Alpe d'Huez and the Grandes Rousses, and given that most readers will be visiting either Alpe d'Huez or one of its satellite stations specifically for a one-week holiday, it would be a shame not to make a point of getting out of your resort for at least a morning to see more of this beautiful region. Having your own vehicle in resort opens up the whole of the Southern Alps, which are home to some major historical towns and cities (Vizille, Briançon, Grenoble) and important international ski stations (Chamrousse, Les Deux Alpes and La Grave, Serre Chevalier and Mongenevre, the latter linked to the Milky Way stations in Italy). These are surrounded by a multitude of further satellite stations and smaller resorts (l'Alpe du Grand Serre, Puy-St-Vincent, Risoul and Les Orres), offering more than enough Alpine pistes, Nordic trails and ski lifts to ensure that you won't cross your own tracks again for weeks on end.

GRANDE GALAXIE

VISALP ski passes of six days or more duration permit a free-of-charge day pass for Puy-St-Vincent, Serre Chevalier/Briançon, The Milky Way (Via Lattea) resorts in Italy and two days at Les Deux Alpes. Les Deux Alpes is easily accessible by shuttle bus from Alpe d'Huez (see page 75 for details); you will need your own vehicle to reach the others. For further information, enquire at the resort:

Ⓦ www.puysaintvincent.com   ☏ +33 (0)4 92 23 35 80
Ⓦ www.serre-chevalier.com   ☏ +33 (0)4 92 24 98 98
Ⓦ www.vialattea.it   ☏ +39 (0)122 79 94 11
Ⓦ www.les2alpes.com   ☏ +33 (0)4 76 79 22 00

LOCAL TRANSPORT

As well as the weekly shuttle between Alpe d'Huez and Les Deux Alpes (see page 75), there are several buses per day from Alpe d'Huez to le-Bourg-d'Oisans and Grenoble; a free shuttle from Oz-en-Oisans Station to the nearby villages of Oz-en-Oisans and Allemont; plus free buses from Vaujany to Allemont and le-Bourg-d'Oisans. From le-Bourg-d'Oisans, there are a number of buses daily to Grenoble via the Chateau de Vizille. For further details, enquire at the tourist offices or contact the transport company Agence VFD ❶ +33 (0)4 76 80 31 60 ❼ www.vfd.fr

LE BOURG-D'OISANS

The capital of the Oisans, only 13 km (8 miles) from Alpe d'Huez, this is an attractive Alpine town with a good range of local shops and an interesting museum of Alpine minerals, crystals and fauna: Musée des minéraux et de la faune des Alpes (small admission charge). ❶ +33 (0)4 76 80 27 54 ❼ www.oisans.com/musee.bo

CHÂTEAU DE VIZILLE

The site of a historic regional assembly meeting on 21 July 1788, whereby the assembly ratified a resolution that registered disapproval at King Louis XVI's meddling in politics and demanded recognition of individual freedom for all French citizens. The King reacted by banning all regional assemblies, helping to trigger the French Revolution. The Château de Vizille is therefore regarded as a cradle of the Revolution and houses France's only specialized museum dedicated to this period of French history, which is located south-east of Grenoble, just 32 km (20 miles) from le-Bourg-d'Oisans via the N91 road.
❼ www.musee-revolution-francaise.fr

ALPE D'HUEZ IN SUMMER

It may never have occurred to you before to visit a ski resort in summer; after all what is there to do after the snow has melted? Quite a lot actually. The mountains are just as beautiful and even more accessible in summer and the glaciers are still open for skiing throughout the high summer months. Away from the glaciers, many other ski lifts also reopen during July and August to transport hikers, mountaineers and mountain bikers to the high ridges and peaks. The majority of the pistes may be green in colour now that the snow has gone, but the routes of the blue, red and black pistes still carry those gradings for downhill mountain biking – pointing your wheels rather than your ski tips or board down the fall line takes just as much skill and guts. Horse riding, white-water sports, quadbiking and rock climbing are just some of the other ways summer visitors get their kicks.

● *The summer face of Alpe d'Huez*

The après jour in the resort bars and restaurants may be more mellow than the après ski in winter, but there are still rocking venues if you know where to look.

To escape from the stressful pace of modern life demands a much more sophisticated alternative to the standard 'fly & flop' beach holiday, so why not try the natural active high offered by the mountains in summer?

SUMMER SPORTS & EVENTS

From early July to the beginning of September, the Pic Blanc cable car carries die-hard snowsports enthusiasts up to the Glacier de Sarenne to participate in summer skiing, just one of more than 60 activities offered by Alpe d'Huez during the summer months. The resort is home to the Poutran International Equestrian Centre and also

◆ *The Maxiavalanche Mountain Bike race on the Glacier de Sarenne*

hosts several other major international sporting events.

The 21 bends on the D211 road up to Alpe d'Huez are a legendary stage on the Tour de France. Every July, the Tour media circus flies in and the resort is packed to capacity with race support teams and the masses of spectators who line the route. Driving up this hill is exhausting enough, but spare a thought for the athletes who cycle up – at the end of a full day's racing! Book well in advance if you want to visit during this period.

Another major two-wheeled event is the Maxiavalanche Mountain Bike race. From a massed start on the summit of Pic Blanc, the competitors ride over the glacier and then all the way down the route of the Sarenne run, through the Gorge de Sarenne to the finishing point deep in the valley.

Details of all summer activities and special events are advertised on the resorts' summer websites. Find links to them at
Ⓦ **www.ski-ride.com** in the summer months.

GLOSSARY

Alpine skiing: the proper name for the sport of Downhill skiing, where participants use gravity to descend the slopes; as opposed to propelling themselves along.

Arête: a sharp ridge separating two glacial valleys or cirques.

Base station: the main access point and ski lifts departure point for a particular ski area; ideally the resort itself.

Base lodge: the main services building at the base station.

Bucket lift: a type of gondola lift where passengers stand in a basic open cabin, usually installed in hilly resort centres and lower slopes areas as public transport from one sector to another.

Button lift: a type of ski lift which consists of a pole hanging from the haul cable, fitted with a circular 'button' that is placed between your legs to pull you uphill.

Carver: a type of ski that is much wider at the tips (front) and tails (rear), allowing for wide, exaggerated turns on the piste.

Cirque: a semi-circular sweep of steep mountains surrounding a generally flat high-altitude valley; a product of glacial erosion.

Couloir: a steep and usually narrow gully sometimes called a chute.

Declutchable chair lift: the fastest type of chair lift, which disconnects from the fast haul cable at the passenger get-on and get-off points to allow for easier mount/dismount.

Drag lift: generic name for all ski lifts that pull passengers along whilst they are standing on the snow.

FIS: Fédération Internationale de Ski (International Ski Federation). The governing body of snowsports, which sets rules and regulations for piste safety and international competitions.

Freeride: a form of skiing away from the pistes where participants ride wherever and however the terrain (usually extreme) allows.

Funicular: a type of railway, usually steeply inclined.

Gondola lift: a type of ski lift where passengers ride inside a small cabin. Also called a Télécabine or Telecabina in Europe; smaller versions are also known as 'bubble lifts'.

Halfpipe: a specially prepared, semi-circular, pisted trough allowing users to ride up its high side walls to perform tricks.

Kickers: ramps of snow which provide a launch point for jumping high into the air.

Langlauf: the correct term for cross-country/Nordic-style skiing where skiers propel themselves in a walking or skating motion; Langlauf skis are much longer and narrower than Alpine skis.

Magic carpet: a conveyor belt.

Mogul (mogul field): bump (series of bumps) formed after heavy use of a ski slope has left the slope deeply rutted; advanced riders relish the challenge of riding through/over these bumps.

Monoskiing: a single large ski where binding attachments are side-by-side and close together.

Nordic skiing: see Langlauf

Nursery slope: a gentle slope designated as a beginners' area.

Off-piste: skiing/snowboarding away from the prepared ski slopes.

Piste: a way-marked slope/trail, where the snow has been groomed to make it easier to ski on. Pistes are graded by difficulty and colour coded to reflect this: green runs are the easiest; blue runs are slightly more challenging but still relatively easy; red runs are difficult slopes requiring technical ability from users; black pistes are the most difficult slopes reserved for expert users.

Piste basher: a tracked snowplough vehicle, fitted with a large rake with which to groom the pistes.

Rope tow: a basic ski lift consisting of a simple loop of rope, where users just grab on to be pulled along.

Schuss: the onomatopoeic term for skiing fast down a straight slope.

Ski-Doo: trade name for a snowmobile; a tracked vehicle fitted with steerable skis resembling a motorbike.

Ski school: the generic term for an organization which provides snowsports tuition.

Slalom: a form of skiing/snowboarding involving weaving in and out of a series of spaced poles/gates, normally against the clock.

Snow Park: a specially designated area set out with ramps (kickers), halfpipes and high rails for sliding along for performing tricks.

Snowshoe: a specialized form of footwear which spreads the wearer's weight over a greater surface area, making it easier to walk over snow.

Telemark skiing: an old form of classic Alpine skiing where the skier's foot is secured to the ski binding only at the toe end, requiring the skier to flex their ankle and knee to effect turns.

Tool point: a collection of spanners and screwdrivers at a designated location on the mountain, provided to allow experienced skiers/snowboarders to adjust their own equipment.

EMERGENCIES

Emergency contact telephone numbers:

Piste security/assistance:	+33 (0)4 76 80 37 38
Medical emergencies	15
Fire	18
Police (Gendarmerie)	Alpe d'Huez +33 (0)4 76 80 32 44
	le-Bourg-d'Oisans +33 (0)4 76 80 00 17
Hospital (Grenoble)	+33 (0)4 76 76 75 75

In the event of a serious accident:

1. Secure the area – plant skis in the form of an 'X' slightly above the position of any casualties, or have someone stand there to warn slope traffic; protect the victim from further injury.

2. First aid – ascertain the condition of the casualty and the extent of any injuries. Administer first aid only if you know what you are doing. Make sure the victim is kept warm and reassured.

A warm drink will help, but ONLY if the person has been fully conscious throughout; never give alcohol.

- If a limb appears to be fractured, protect it from further movement.
- If the casualty is unconscious, check to see that he or she is breathing; if not, start artificial respiration immediately.
- Place the casualty in the recovery position: gently roll the person on to his or her side, head down to prevent choking.

3. Alert the nearest station personnel and/or the piste patrol/emergency services. Make a note of the name/number of the nearest piste marker.

4. Exchange names and contact details with all parties to the accident, including witnesses and station personnel.

5. Get the casualty to shelter as soon as it is safe to move them.

PICTURE CREDITS

The publisher would like to thank the following for permission to reproduce their photographs: **Office du Tourisme de l'Alpe d'Huez** – pp 1, 3, 56, 101, 104, 232, 237 (V. Thiebaut-Thuria) and pp 4, 240, 250, 251 (J. P. Noisillier – Agence NUTS); **Comité Départemental du Tourisme de l'Isère** p 15 (E. Lecocq); **Stephen Corporon** pp 12, 24, 28, 35; **Phillip Simpson** pp 154, 167, 170; **Sofia Barbas** p 78. Original piste map artwork by **Frederique and Pierre Novat**.